# TRIAL JUDGE: A JOB DESCRIPTION

## OR

## ELEVEN AND A HALF YEARS ON THE BENCH

Robert K. Young

**Lehigh Valley, Pennsylvania**

**2018**

# DEDICATED TO THE
## COMMONWEALTH OF PENNSYLVANIA

Any net proceeds from the sale of this book will be donated to Pennsylvania charities, or non-profit organizations.

To Muhlenberg President Williams - 12/11/18
Thank you for your time and ideas regarding the Kalmbach Estate. Pages 193-194 of this book should provide you with a sketchy background.
Best wishes in your important new job.
Bob Young

TABLE OF CONTENTS

A Note About Legal Writing and Punctuation ............................................................................. v

Introduction .................................................................................................................................... 1

Memo to My Great-Grandchildren ................................................................................................. 2

Gittinger's Plan .............................................................................................................................. 3

Great-Grandchild #5 ...................................................................................................................... 3

Key to the Court House .................................................................................................................. 5

Parking the Caddy .......................................................................................................................... 7

The Court's Jurisdiction ................................................................................................................. 8

Barbara vs. Matchmaker International .......................................................................................... 10

Estate of Terrance L. Reiss: Was he Married? ............................................................................ 14

Court Administrator, Susan T. Schellenberg and the Expansion of Family Court ...................... 21

A Custody Case: Philip vs. Linda ................................................................................................ 22

Juvenile Court: Delinquency and Adjudication ........................................................................... 26

Gotthardt vs. Molloy .................................................................................................................... 27

The Private Nature of Judging ..................................................................................................... 39

A Judge's Staff: Court Crier, Secretary, Law Clerk, Deputy Sheriff, Tipstaff ........................... 40

Jan Thwaites and Barbara Yost ................................................................................................... 42

Choosing Law Clerks ................................................................................................................... 43

Swearing in Jurors ........................................................................................................................ 43

Court Reporters ............................................................................................................................ 44

No Gavel, No Raising Funds ........................................................................................................ 44

Keeping Silent .............................................................................................................................. 45

The Semi-Annual Judicial Conferences and the National Judicial College ................................ 45

St. Luke's "Right to Die" Case ................................................................................................ 47

Electric Shock Treatments ...................................................................................................... 48

N.E.S. "Right to Die" Case ..................................................................................................... 49

The Estate of M. K.: A Homeless Lady Found to be Incapacitated ......................................... 54

The State Hospital Situation ................................................................................................... 63

The Kalmbach Estate: A New Park .......................................................................................... 64

Dr. Scheie: "Over Reaching" ................................................................................................... 65

Court Assignments: Criminal Court ......................................................................................... 67

Sentencing is Almost an Art .................................................................................................... 68

The Harvey Robinson Appeal ................................................................................................... 70

The Placement of Law Clerks .................................................................................................. 71

The Snow Tracks Case ............................................................................................................. 71

A Case of Jury Nullification ..................................................................................................... 72

The O'Neal vs. Osborne Case:  An Automobile Collision ........................................................ 73

Lear vs. Hartman ..................................................................................................................... 78

A Waste of the Court's Time .................................................................................................... 82

The City of Allentown Tax Levy Case ...................................................................................... 82

Where do Cases Go on Appeal? ............................................................................................... 87

"Taking Judicial Notice": Lower Macungie Township Reclassification ..................................... 88

A Word or Two About "Argument Court" ................................................................................. 90

A Zoning Board Appeal:  Toth vs. Allentown Zoning Board ..................................................... 91

Motion Court: Petitions and  Protection From Abuse Cases ..................................................... 98

The Hospital Cases ................................................................................................................... 100

Naturalization Court ................................................................................................................. 103

Election Day Duties ............................................................................................ 104

A Judge Cannot Say "I Don't Know" .................................................................. 105

On Lawyers:  Their Importance and Temperament ............................................. 106

A Tax Assessment Case: Mack Trucks vs. County of Lehigh .............................. 108

HAB Industries vs. City of Allentown: Business Privilege Tax on Manufacturing, or was it
     Processing? ................................................................................................... 116

Toll Brothers, Inc. vs. South Whitehall Township ............................................. 122

Slip and Fall:  Holly Kohler vs. Herbert Hyman ............................................... 130

Medical Malpractice:  The High/Low Concept .................................................. 139

Jury Trials ........................................................................................................... 146

Lawsuits Against Professionals:  The Halperin Case ......................................... 148

And Next, a Teacher's Termination: ................................................................... 153

The Whistleblower Case ..................................................................................... 162

Sovereign Immunity............................................................................................ 170

Products Liability: Snyder vs. Fruehauf ............................................................. 186

LARA vs. Dorney Park Coaster Company .......................................................... 193

A Bench Trial:  Erie Insurance vs. McBride....................................................... 194

A Shocking Jury Verdict..................................................................................... 201

A Short Explanation of Post Trial Relief............................................................ 208

Child Support:  Domestic Relations Section Cases ........................................... 223

Judicial Restraint................................................................................................. 224

The Cases I Disliked, the Cases I Liked ............................................................. 225

Adoptions............................................................................................................ 227

Afterthoughts ...................................................................................................... 228

A Point for Charge for my Great-Grandchildren................................................ 230

Biographical Note About the Author ........................................................................... 231

Acknowledgements ..................................................................................................... 232

Appendix ..................................................................................................................... 233

Index of Names ........................................................................................................... 234

# A NOTE ABOUT LEGAL WRITING AND PUNCTUATION

Some readers may question what seems to be arbitrarily capitalized words throughout this book. Capitalization in legal writing is controlled by Rule 8 of *The Bluebook, A Uniform System of Citation.* Words not capitalized in other writing styles are capitalized in legal writing to emphasize the relationship of a person to the case being discussed.

The titles of legal documents are to be capitalized unless you are referring to a generic category of documents. Legal writers follow special rules about when to capitalize names of courts, judges, government offices, plaintiff/defendant and other terms. For example:

- Plaintiff has disputed the terms of the Last Will and Testament of Arthur Smith. Smith met with his attorney to draft a new will on the 19th of January, 2014.

- Attorneys file complaints, answers, petitions and motions on paper unless electronic filing is permitted.

- Today the Court examines the Motion for Special Relief of the Plaintiff Mildred Pearce. In many cases, motions like this made by a plaintiff are granted. In the case, Jack vs. Jill, plaintiff filed a motion asking the court to grant him exclusive possession of the hill upon which the married couple lived.

The style, grammar, punctuation and vocabulary used in legal drafting, while no longer a perplexing jargon of Latin and arcane English, is often passive and employs the use of many dependent and independent clauses. There are some words that are used nearly exclusively in legal writing, (demurrer, voir dire, docket, movant, etc.) and some words that have a very specific legal meaning different that the most common usage (motion, answer, count, damages, discovery, finding, etc.) *The Bluebook* is available online at www.legalbluebook.com.

# INTRODUCTION

This book is a first-person account describing and explaining the work performed, and many of the issues confronted, by a Pennsylvania Trial Judge. Although it is primarily addressed to my Great-Grandchildren, it is my hope that the included material will be of interest to others. I'm sure that some of the local barristers will enjoy it, and I am fairly sure that some of the local judges will have disagreements with several of my theories. I am most hopeful that teachers and professors may find value in the book to acquaint their students with the civic issues contained in it, and to learn a little about the amazing, productive, useful, and interesting aspects of our American judicial system.

One problem in trying to reach such a diverse audience is how to keep the work simple for those who will just like to read some of the stories contained in my narrative, and yet provide enough case law to show, (a) the wide variety of disputes that need solving, (b) the differing types of courts that have evolved, and, (c) an example of the temper of a typical trial judge through his written opinions. I want more cases; my editor wants fewer.

We discussed the possibility of producing a "Student" edition, and a second "Abridged" one, but came to an agreement that I would remove a few more cases, and that I would write this introduction advising anyone who feels bogged down by absorbing the details of the law, to skip the cases without guilt and move on.

# MEMO TO MY GREAT-GRANDCHILDREN

To: My Great-Grandchildren and Other Curious People
From: Judge Young
Date: 2018, in my 87<sup>th</sup> year
Subject: My Judging Job

I never knew any of my great grandparents. I often wonder what they actually did from day-to-day to make a living. I want you to know about me and what it was like to be a trial judge. Your parents and grandparents can fill you in on the basic facts about my education, personality, interests and good looks. There are several lawyers in our family who can describe the workings of that profession in which I served for about 27 years before I captured a judgeship.

My hope is that at some point in your lives, (probably when you are in your twenties or thirties) you will acquire an interest in knowing what your great grandfather did "on the bench," and what he thought about during that time. Reading some of my Orders and Opinions should disclose most of the nature of my work during those eleven and a half years on the bench.

# GITTINGER'S PLAN

I believe that it was Christopher Gittinger, who survived a two-year sentence as my first law clerk, who started keeping a file that contained copies of those of my Orders and Opinions that were appealed to a higher court. "Orders" are just short statements of the results of a case. "Opinions" may be in the form of a footnote or a more detailed discussion of the reasons behind the Order which the parties and public are entitled to know.

When the Superior or Commonwealth Courts handed down their respective Judgments as to whether or not my decisions were proper, Chris put them in the file after reading them. The other clerks who followed Chris kept up that process until my retirement in early 1996. Several months ago, for no particular reason, I decided to browse through that heavy file. It contained 71 separate cases. Those, and all of my other hundreds of decisions are contained in the files of the different courthouse offices.

# GREAT-GRANDCHILD #5

Shortly after putting the file back in an old chest, Carolyn, my wife, and I learned that we had just acquired our fifth great grandchild, the oldest of which was less than two years old. (There were several mothers involved in this production.) The new baby was, of course, more than welcome, but the thought came to me that I, at 87 years old, was never going to really know those heirs. When they got to the age of 10, I would be 97. Not much chance – and how sharp would my mind then be?

I thought about talking to them through a Blog, stored for posterity somewhere in the "Cloud." Perhaps an oral history cut onto a CD, or even a DVD produced by a professional studio. We have a scrapbook with photos, but looking at someone else's prints has not been too interesting when that duty has been assigned to me.

My job as a trial judge was exciting. I want to share that excitement with you, and perhaps with other people who are interested in what one trial judge actually did and thought. The best way to do that will be to let people read my decisions on the problematic cases of my judgeship, scatter my comments throughout, and end with my conclusions. You will be happy to learn that I have culled the 71 cases down to 28. Think of them as real life short stories. They are.

What I was doing as a trial judge was in no way unique. In June of 2017, there were 422 trial judges in Pennsylvania. The numbers change as judges retire, die, take senior status, and as new judgeships are created. But I was one of that 400 or so judges. Of course, no other judge had identical cases, but we were all working to serve the system of resolving the legal issues between individuals, corporations and local governments. Judges do not work alone. Later, I will be describing the support staff that is needed to maximize a judge's productivity.

## Trial Judge:  A Job Description

This might be a good place to tell you how I became a trial judge. I'll quote from some written remarks that I passed on to my University of Pennsylvania Law School classmates at our 50th reunion.

When I started practicing law in 1956 in Lehigh County we had about 150 members of our Bar Association. (Now, over 600.) Of course, we all knew each other, and times were more relaxed. There was a regular luncheon table (about 15 seats) at the fine hotel a block away from the Court House. Usually two or three of our four judges came to eat with us (or we with them). This went on for years.

After a lot of lunches where I was exposed to a great deal of friendly wisdom, I decided somewhere in the 70's that I would like to be a Lehigh County Judge. When a vacancy occurred, I ran for the position, but came in second in a field of seven. Not long after my oldest son became an attorney, and for about seven years, he and I had a great time practicing together. What a pleasure to watch a son mature into a good lawyer.

Then another vacancy came along in about 1983, due to an early retirement for health reasons. I had no strong feelings about putting in my name to fill the year and a half left until the next election, because things were going along so well on all fronts. I remember that my son and I were eating at a local Arby's one day and he, having helped in my first campaign, thought it would be a good idea to try for the nomination by the Governor. What was there to lose, and he felt confident about keeping our practice going whether for the short time or longer if I won the election.

Again, four or five other local lawyers wanted to be a judge, and all of us prepared the usual resumes and were interviewed in Harrisburg, not by the Governor, but by two of his "appointment secretaries." For reasons still not entirely known to me, I was told at the interview that I would be nominated by Governor Thornburgh. Along with a good Montgomery County Democrat, (I being a not so good Republican) I was quickly confirmed by the Senate.

Being the incumbent, I won both tickets in the Primary and served for a total of eleven and a half years. It was a great way to end my career. The change of jobs really stretched my brain, and the work seemed useful.

# KEY TO THE COURT HOUSE

A day or two after I was sworn in, the Court Administrator handed me a key to the Courthouse. The key opened the outside and inside doors, except for the door to the District Attorney's evidence room. I had never thought about the key. It produced a tingle of excitement, knowing then that I really was a judge. The only little problem was that I did not have a permanently assigned courtroom. For over five years, I would learn on a weekly (and sometimes daily) basis where there was a vacant room. I often held court in an oversized conference room with just a table and chairs, no bench. Other times the huge front courtroom across Fifth Street in the Old Courthouse was available, and when Federal District Judge Edward N. Cahn was sitting in Philadelphia he let me use the rear courtroom of the Old Courthouse. I was able to use the courtrooms of the other judges when they were on vacation, or when they had an office week. Rain or shine, we had to carry my robe and materials wherever we were assigned.

**From left to right: Mike Brocshack, Tipstaff; Angelo Almonti, Law Clerk; Edie Schwoyer, Crier; Me; and Matt Giovannini, Court Reporter.**

The lawyers, sheriffs, court clerks and court reporters had to check with the court administrator's office at each change of venue. It really was not too onerous, but the reporter for *The Morning Call* had fun with the story and ran a big article about my travels, complete with a photo of myself and my staff crossing Fifth Street.

I was eventually given my own handsome, paneled courtroom, complete with a spacious office and jury room to use. I did sneak in two improvements on weekends. I installed a modest speaker system in the courtroom, complete with a small lapel microphone that I could attach to the collar of my robe, but I had to be careful to click it off at sidebar conferences. (That is when the lawyers and the judge huddle together at the bench to debate a point of law that the jury or others in the courtroom are not supposed to hear.) I also added a telephone jack in the jury room that was regularly used for settlement or pre-trial conferences, adoptions, etc.

I wonder if my Great-Grandchildren know why a telephone jack is needed. They may have a communication device wired into their brains by the time they read this. They will surely not appreciate the skill of being able to make seven or even eight copies of a typewritten letter by using sheets of thin carbon paper. Perhaps an old movie will show them what was my ultimate office machine – an IBM Selectric typewriter that printed with a magical spinning ball. We dictated most correspondence to a secretary who could write "shorthand." Voice recognition was unheard of.

# PARKING THE CADDY

A long with the courthouse key came a remote garage door opener. We, my secretary Barbara and I, both had parking spaces in the courthouse basement. That was a big deal, but in my case called for some cautious driving. The courthouse is situated on land that is prone to limestone sinkholes. The architect had placed very large cement support columns fairly close together, which left rather narrow lanes to negotiate a car to its assigned spot. I was commuting using a 1967 four-door Cadillac. (The car was a second-hand gift in 1987 from my five children.) At over eighteen feet long it was a challenge to park. I never hit anything, and was often congratulated by other nervous tenants. I still have the 50-year-old car, hoping it might last for the next three generations of mine. I warn, however, that it only gets nine miles to a high-test gallon.

*Sharon K. Merkel of Images.*
**The 1967 Cadillac I used every day to commute to the Court House. Although a birthday gift to me from my children, it has been a bit expensive to maintain. I purchased and cannibalized a "parts car," so there is a good chance that it will last a generation or so.**

# THE COURT'S JURISDICTION

## PENNSYLVANIA COURT OF COMMON PLEAS

### Hearing Court
- Non-jury matters that require testimony such as tax assessment cases & injunctions
- Suppression Hearings
- Summary Appeals

### Argument Court
- Any legal issue arising out of any case
- No testimony-must be briefed
- Zoning
- Wrongful Discharge

### Motion Court
- Miscellaneous petitions for example: To continue case, to change name, to grant new trial, to stay sheriff's sale, to issue Protection From Abuse Order, etc. See text

### Criminal Court
- Trials by jury or judge
- Summary offences
- Misdemeanors & Felonies
- Bail
- Search & Seizure
- Fines & Costs
- Condition of Probation
- Guilty Pleas
- Sentencing
- Habeas Corpus
- Work release
- Restitution
- Community Service

**YOU**

**ALL DIVISIONS AND COURTS**

### Family Court
- Child and Spousal Support
- Child Custody
- Divorce
- Property Division

### Orphans' Court
- Decedents' estates
- Wills
- Adoptions
- Guardianships
- Incapacitated
- Minors
- Trusts
- By-pass hearings
- Right-to-die
- Non-profits
- Cemeteries

### Juvenile Court
- Delinquency hearings
- Adjudications
- Placement
- Community Service
- Dependency Hearings

### Civil Court
- Medical Malpractice
- Contract Disputes
- Negligence
- Product Liability
- Fraud
- Libel & Defamation

Argument, Hearing, and Motions Courts serve the needs of the five official divisions (underlined). There are additional ceremonial courts such as Naturalization, Bar Memorials and Judicial Installations. The list of case types are illustrative and are not complete.
Pennsylvania Court of Common Pleas Chart © 2017 Robert K. Young

I have prepared and included this chart to provide an overview of the extensive scope of the Court's work. Pennsylvania's Courts of Common Pleas have almost unlimited jurisdiction over legal disputes assigned to them. Each of the State's 67 Counties has a Court of Common Pleas, although in a few rural areas two Counties share one Court. The designation "Common Pleas" comes to us from England. Those cases were ones where the British Sovereign allowed its common citizens to sue each other.

Lawsuits involving matters that seek less than $50,000 are taken first to an Arbitration Panel, on which three local attorneys sit as arbitrators. The biggest load off of Common Pleas Judges' shoulders is handled by our Magisterial District Judges. They have concurrent jurisdiction with Common Pleas to hear matters up to $12,000 involving Landlord/Tenant disputes, negligence cases, contract actions and municipal ordinance violations. In criminal cases, the District Judges issue subpoenas, search and arrest warrants, emergency Protection From Abuse Orders, and set bail. They also conduct preliminary hearings and try summary cases such as disorderly conduct and traffic offenses. Magisterial District Judges do not need to be attorneys, but are required to attend regular educational seminars relating to their responsibilities. Our Common Pleas Court Judges could not possibly handle all that Magisterial District Judges do and keep up with the volume of their present workload.

The Magisterial District Judges, the Common Pleas Judges and the Appellate Court Judges are State officers, paid by the State. The Legislature sets their annual compensation, payable monthly, and their medical and pension benefits. I found the pay and benefits very reasonable—particularly the three-week vacation. The State, when I was serving, also paid the County $90,000 to help defer the cost to the County for providing court facilities and staff to each judge. That sum was completely inadequate. On the other hand, the judges were, for the most part, deciding legal problems that were occurring in the County. It was the County's residents who were being served.

Sometimes a case never gets to be fully heard and decided on its merits. If you want to use the court system to determine a dispute, you must start by filing a Complaint. A Complaint sets forth the facts of the matter in detail, point by point. After reading that document, the judge may conclude that the plaintiff does not really have a viable case. An example of that process follows.

# BARBARA VS. MATCHMAKER INTERNATIONAL

IN THE COURT OF COMMON PLEAS OF LEHIGH COUNTY, PENNSYLVANIA

CIVIL ACTION - LAW

BARBARA                              )
                                     )
          Plaintiff                  )
                                     )
     vs.                             )   No. 88-C-2911
                                     )
MATCHMAKER INTERNATIONAL,            )
                                     )
          Defendant                  )

## ORDER

NOW, this 7ᵗ day of August, 1992, after review of the Pleadings, Briefs, and entire Record in the above-captioned matter,

IT IS ORDERED that the Preliminary Objections of the Defendant in the nature of a demurrer are Sustained.[1]

BY THE COURT:

*Robert K. Young*
Robert K. Young, Judge

---

[1]If the courts were not so busy, this case would generate a full-blown Opinion. It seems that the Plaintiff (Barbara) decided to improve her social life by engaging the services of the Defendant (Matchmaker). Barbara wished to establish a meaningful relationship with a compatible male

CONTINUATION OF FOOTNOTE

---

companion. Based upon Matchmaker's representation that it carefully screened and interviewed all of its members, Barbara joined Matchmaker's Personal Introduction Service for a fee of $395.00.

While the first prospect was unacceptable, Barbara did enter into a very "meaningful" liaison with "Paul" who was introduced to her by Matchmaker on September 10, 1985. They continued their togetherness until April of 1987. The break-up resulted, alleges Barbara, from the fact that Paul not only continued to borrow money from her, but that he also fraudulently used her credit cards. She now asks the use of the Court to recover her lost money (approximately $4,000.00) _from Matchmaker_. Furthermore, she seeks monetary damages from Matchmaker for the severe emotional distress that she suffered, as well as damages for the loss of her job.

Judges must be patient and respectful and, thus, Barbara and her Counsel are entitled to review the reasoning for throwing them out of Court.

       (1)   Barbara claims that Matchmaker broke its contract with her, in that it must have failed to screen Paul's character. She leaps to the conclusion that a screening process is equivalent to a performance guarantee. Matchmaker never entered into a contract warranting the performance of its members.

       (2)   Barbara further puts forth the legal principle that she is entitled to money from Matchmaker because it negligently screened Paul's character. She offers no facts to support the causal connection between an alleged failure to screen and Paul's

-2-

CONTINUATION OF FOOTNOTE

_____

subsequent misdeeds; only stating that he damaged her.  A loss does not establish liability.

(3)  Barbara also relies on a violation of the Pennsylvania Unfair Trade Practices and Consumer Protection Law, 73 P.S. §202-2(4), which defines unfair or deceptive acts as:

"Failing to comply with the written terms of any guarantee or warranty given to the buyer at, prior to, or after the contract for the purpose of goods or services is made..."

Matchmaker did not guarantee its members' performance. Its function was to bring people together, not keep them together.

(4)  Barbara's suit also includes a claim for misrepresentation. She provides no details regarding the lack of screening by Matchmaker, which was the only representation which is relied upon by her. Matchmaker did not represent the moral integrity of all of its members.

The courts are designed to help citizens fulfill their reasonable expectations.  If a wrong has been done to an individual which disturbs the flow of his or her life, the courts are here.  But no one can reasonably expect a guarantee of happiness; only its pursuit.  Matchmaker represented that it screened their referrals.  No reasonable

-3-

CONTINUATION OF FOOTNOTE

_____

person would thus believe that a lifetime guarantee of love, fidelity, and honesty was being made. Humans are notoriously unpredictable. They are subject to innumerable pressures. Barbara's life has undoubtedly been badly disrupted by her encounter with Paul, but she must look elsewhere than Matchmaker for relief.

Note the use of a footnote to explain my decision. That was my preferred time-saving practice, and the appellate courts were never critical of it. The Matchmaker case was not appealed, but probably because it is such an appeal—able story, someone put it among the only copies of cases that I took home at retirement.

-4-

# ESTATE OF TERRANCE L. REISS: WAS HE MARRIED?

The next example of the kinds of matters that came before me to resolve was The Estate of Terrance L. Reiss, Deceased. I used an Opinion to explain my finding, not a footnote. I was affirmed by the Superior Court. (For future reference, unless I indicate that the appellate court reversed my holdings, consider them affirmed). I have retained the citations to other cases that contained precedent for the sake of authenticity and to indicate how much work was involved in researching. I have redacted the full names of a few litigants where I was concerned about bringing embarrassment or mental pain. All of the reported cases occurred twenty to thirty years ago, and in most instances, were tried in open court. At the time that they were written, there was no thought about using them as examples for my heirs or anyone else.

The Reiss Estate introduces the part of my judge's job that requires me to decide who is telling the truth. It was a non-jury case, which is almost always the practice in the Orphans' Court. We hardly ever use the word "lying," and instead indicate that the witness was "not credible." However, judges know that humans often believe what they want to believe, and are sometimes honestly mistaken. In those cases, we try to look at any other evidence that might corroborate or contradict what a particular witness is telling us.

IN THE COURT OF COMMON PLEAS OF LEHIGH COUNTY, PENNSYLVANIA

ORPHANS' COURT DIVISION

IN RE:                          )
                                )
    ESTATE OF                   )
                                )  File No. 1990-1124
        TERRANCE L. REISS,      )
                                )
            DECEASED            )

* * * * *

APPEARANCES:

> DIANNE M. DICKSON, ESQUIRE,
> And with her, WORTH LAW OFFICES, P.C.,
>> On behalf of the Estate of Terrance L. Reiss,
>> also known as Terry L. Reiss, Deceased.

> CLYDE O. BARTEL, ESQUIRE,
>> On behalf of Lance John Lee Reiss, a Minor.

> ELISSA J. GRIFFITH, ESQUIRE,
> And with her, HUBER, WALDRON & GRIFFITH,
>> On behalf of Cynthia E. Rotenberger.

> KEVIN T. FOGERTY, ESQUIRE,
> And with him, TRAUB, BUTZ & FOGERTY, P.C.,
>> On behalf of Norman R. Reiss and Margaret M.
>> Reiss.

* * * * *

OPINION

ROBERT K. YOUNG, Judge.

This Opinion becomes necessary due to the appeal

-1-

of a finding by this Court that the Decedent, Terrance L. Reiss, and the Appellant, Cynthia E. Rotenberger, were not husband and wife at the time of the death of Mr. Reiss (Terry). The matter is of some importance. Terry died intestate and if Ms. Rotenberger (Cynthia) was his wife, she will inherit the major portion of his estate. Otherwise, the estate will pass to Terry's son, Lance, a minor, who is also the son of Cynthia. The Court has also decided, following a full Hearing, that Lance was Terry's son.

The testimony regarding the marital status of Terry and Cynthia was intertwined with the testimony having to do with the paternity of Lance. Cynthia acknowledges that there was no formal marriage ceremony. Her claim rests upon a common-law status. In view of that fact it is incumbent upon her to convince the fact finder by clear and convincing evidence. In re Estate of Kovalchick, 345 Pa.Super. 229, 498 A.2d 374 (1985). Because of the following findings of fact, the Court has great doubt that a marriage relationship existed.

The couple met in September of 1982. They began to live together shortly thereafter. Cynthia became pregnant in the Summer of 1984. The couple lived with

Terry's parents for approximately three months. They planned for a wedding at that time, but Terry's parents insisted upon a Catholic ceremony, which was not the wish of Terry and Cynthia. Cynthia left the Reiss home (Terry's parents) and moved to Quakertown with her mother. Terry stayed with his parents.

The couple moved back together in the Fall of 1984, into an apartment in Emmaus, Pennsylvania. Lance was born April 25, 1985. After the birth of Lance, Terry and Cynthia lived together "off and on", and sometime in 1985 Terry left. In October of 1987, Terry and Cynthia bought a home in joint names in Slatington, Pennsylvania. That deed placed the title in their names as "joint tenants with the right of survivorship". Terry moved out of that home in April of 1988 to resume residency with his parents. However, before he left, he and Cynthia entered into a Non Marital Cohabitation and Property Agreement. That Agreement, dated February 4, 1988, which was prepared by Counsel and signed by Cynthia (and Terry) states that:

WHEREAS, the parties to this Agreement are an unmarried man and woman who desire to live together sharing the same residence.

WHEREAS, the parties are both gainfully employed and desire to pursue their respective careers during the course of their relationship; and

WHEREAS, the parties specifically intend not to enter into a marriage agreement under either ceremonial or commonlaw;

The above-noted "Non Marital" Agreement was followed by a Complaint in Equity wherein Terry sued Cynthia in an action in Equity, specifically averring that the parties were unmarried. Cynthia admitted in her Answer that she and Terry were unmarried. A few days later Cynthia sued Terry for Specific Performance, Partition, and Breach of Warranty. Cynthia also pled New Matter. The essence of that litigation was to enforce the Non Marital Agreement. Cynthia also brought a Petition for Protection from Abuse against Terry in which she alleged, under oath, that Terry was her "ex-boyfriend".

Cynthia claims that she and Terry reconciled in the Fall of 1989, although she concedes that they continued to live separately. The Court does not find that testimony credible. The one piece of evidence in her favor is a designation by Terry on an application to his employer's health insurance policy wherein he sought to add Cynthia as a beneficiary. He wrote in her relationship as "his common law wife". This was signed in August of 1990. Further,

-4-

Reverend James Vaughn testified that from March 19, 1990 through September 6, 1990, Terry met with him approximately five times, and indicated that he wished to be married. Reverend Vaughn said that Terry stated that he was the common law husband of Cynthia. The Reverend filled out a form for Social Security benefits, after Terry's death and at Cynthia's request, indicating this common law relationship. Other witnesses testified, including Terry's attorney, his mother and his girlfriend with whom he lived from October of 1988 through the beginning of 1990. All of them stated that Terry did not consider himself married to Cynthia.

The Court has already commented that it did not find most of Cynthia's testimony believable. Evasiveness and inconsistencies permeated her responses. As to Reverend Vaughn, it is conceivable that Terry indicated that he and Cynthia were common law husband and wife. The Reverend was being asked to counsel and marry this couple who were living together at that time, with their child. One such statement to a member of the clergy and one health insurance application does not meet the clear and convincing burden of proof imposed upon the proponent of a common law marriage.

-5-

This is particularly the case when both the man and woman have publicly, under oath and in court proceedings, specifically denied a husband and wife relationship. In prior proceedings Cynthia has invoked the Court's authority on the basis of her single status. We simply do not believe this latest story.

* * * * *

Norman R. Reiss and Margaret M. Reiss have also appealed this Court's Final Decree of January 5, 1993. They are the parents of Terry Reiss. They will inherit Terry's substantial estate if they can establish that Lance is not the son of their son. The Court set forth its reasoning for holding that Lance was the son of Terry in a lengthy footnote to its Final Decree, which footnote is by this reference incorporated into and made a part of this Opinion.

BY THE COURT:

Robert K. Young, Judge

Dated: March 3 , 1993

I did not include the footnote dealing with the paternity issue regarding Terry's son Lance. A birth certificate, court records regarding custody and support, and a written sworn statement by Terry that Lance was his son, left no doubts.

# COURT ADMINISTRATOR, SUSAN T. SCHELLENBERG AND THE EXPANSION OF FAMILY COURT

From an Orphans' Court matter to a family custody matter may seem a bit incongruous, but judges are often assigned cases back-to-back that involve entirely differing propositions of law. When I began my position, there were five judges whose work schedules were handled by a practicing attorney, who was subsequently replaced by a full-time Court Administrator, Susan T. Schellenberg. With degrees in Political Science and Court Administration, plus seven years working in the County's largest law firm, she handled the difficult job of assigning a continuous stream of law suits to a group of very independent judges. By adding mediators, masters, and arbitration panels, our inventory of cases was manageable. After I retired the Commonwealth slowly increased the number of judges assigned to our County, the present count being ten.

One of the areas of caseload expansion was in our Family Court. Although I tried to enjoy my work on that court, I admit that I was often disturbed at the behavior of too many people who demonstrated a desire to hurt their spouses, even at a cost to their children. However, I did come across one of my custody cases that tells a nicer story, but wait until you get to the Louis E. vs. Bonnie P. case. Judge Ford and I (each having large close families) took on Family Court as a team. After a short time, both of us were sorely depressed.

# A CUSTODY CASE: PHILIP VS. LINDA

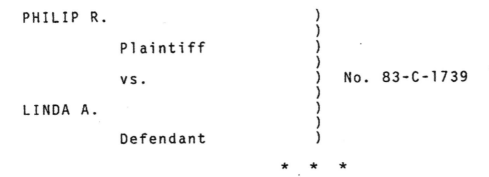

IN THE COURT OF COMMON PLEAS OF LEHIGH COUNTY, PENNSYLVANIA

CIVIL DIVISION - LAW

PHILIP R.                        )
                                 )
          Plaintiff              )
                                 )
          vs.                    )    No. 83-C-1739
                                 )
LINDA A.                         )
                                 )
          Defendant              )

                         *   *   *

APPEARANCES:

          JOHN E. FREUND, III, ESQUIRE,
             And with him, KING, McCARDLE, HERMAN & FREUND,
             On behalf of Plaintiff.

          RICHARD C. BUSS, ESQUIRE,
             And with him, BUSS & LONG,
             On behalf of Defendant.

                         *   *   *


                    O P I N I O N


ROBERT K. YOUNG, Judge.

          We have before us another difficult custody case.

Several full days of Hearings have convinced the Court that

both of the parents of 4-1/2 year old Philip, Junior care
for and love the child. Each parent proposes that he or she
be awarded physical custody of their son during the Winter
months so that he can attend a day-care pre-kindergarten
school, with alternating weekend plus shared holiday visits
being given to the other parent.

The economic and housing aspects of both parents
are very similar, and each has demonstrated adequate concern
for discipline and educational opportunity and achievement.
The father's extended family exhibited a sincere concern and
love for the child, together with a willingness to do all
they can emotionally and financially for the boy. The
mother's mother has recently retired and is anxious to
provide day-long oversight to her grandson while the mother
is working.

In short, the Court finds that both parents are
more than fit to raise their son, and that each parent is
blessed with a fine "support system". Further, we believe
that whatever Order of custody is handed down, that all of
those who have expressed a resolve to help the boy become a
responsible man will continue to love and care for him.

The parties seem to understand that no Court can

-2-

devise an arrangement satisfactory to each of them, and that the prime concern must be for the best interests of their child, given the difficult circumstances brought about by the disintegration of the marriage. To further complicate this matter, the mother has moved to the northern part of New Jersey, which necessitates two long hard drives for the boy and his mother every time a weekend visit occurs under the present circumstances.

The Court met twice in camera with Philip, Junior, in the presence of Counsel, and it is evident that he is a cheerful, normal lad with a great deal of energy. He needs both women and men in his life as he matures. His youth and lack of any extra special needs provides us with the solution upon which we rely. He is both medically and mentally sound (and we do not believe that either parent has abused him). Thus, we shall try to provide him with the affection of all of those who want to help him by dividing his time equally between both parents and their respective families.

The single detriment to this plan is a disruption in the boy's present "education", which consists of a pre-kindergarten program. We are sure that the parents can

-3-

find suitable companion day schools in their respective
areas which will cooperate in providing Philip, Junior with
meaningful and coordinated materials.  Many children of this
age are moved from place to place, and we are not here
dealing with a highly complicated curricula.  The Order to
which this Opinion is appended provides for a review of the
entire situation before the child begins First Grade, and we
will be quite satisfied if this matter can be put on the
right course for a year and a half.  By that time more facts
will be available; Philip, Junior will have matured
considerably; and other attitudes and circumstances of both
parents will probably have changed.  We do not like to
disrupt his pre-kindergarten and kindergarten schooling, but
this is believed better than withholding substantial periods
of custody from either parent.

As the Philip & Linda case demonstrates, custody issues are fluid. Circumstances change. The same fluidity prevails in Support matters. If there are children to support, their needs change as they age. Litigants change jobs, and parties change housing locations, sometimes out of State. People get sick, have accidents and get laid off or fired. The list of items that can upset what was at one time a doable Court Order is long. And too often there were no good solutions. When families break up, they usually must divide, into two parts, resources that before were marginally able to carry along one family unit. But the suffering was real. Medicine was not being taken, rent not paid, food stamps needed and on and on. Thus, I entered the fairest Order I could think of. And what good was the Order? If, for example, the father does not pay the dictated sum due for the support of his wife and children, what options does the Court have? We can scold, threat, fine, or jail. Except to set an example to other fathers, it was counterproductive to put a father in jail where he certainly could not make enough money to pay support, (unless he could keep or obtain a job while on work-release – which was very rare). A fine does not help his family, and just puts him deeper in debt.

# JUVENILE COURT:
# DELINQUENCY AND ADJUDICATION

The very first hour and day of my work on the bench I was assigned to Juvenile Court. The County operated a Juvenile Probation Department. Professional male and female probation officers performed the task of presenting the facts of a case in court. Those officers normally handed me a file that contained narrations of any past incidents, family history, school achievements, etc. The youngster was always present, hopefully with a parent, uncle or some other family member. I did not wear a robe.

Juvenile Hearings are usually closed to the public, and there is no jury. Juvenile court issues are divided into two distinct subjects. First, there was proof needed that the minor was delinquent. That is, that the behavior would have been criminal if committed by an adult. If the juvenile and his family agreed to that, and the "crime" was not serious, the Probation Department officer often worked out a correctional program for the youth, tailored to the offense committed. If there was a dispute concerning whether a crime had occurred, the trial judge listened to all of the available witnesses and made that decision. Only after a finding of Delinquency could the second part of a Hearing go forward, which was the Adjudication. What to do with the juvenile.

I tried to make the punishment fit the crime. If the juvenile had spray-painted a building, part of the plan would be to require him or her to clean up or paint over the area, possibly painting it with a pleasant decoration that the juvenile would not like to have smeared. Community service was used extensively. Curfews, loss of biking privileges, coming directly home from school, helping with home chores and baby-sitting siblings were a few favorites when dealing with minor infractions.

I recall one community service that was ordered by another judge. Four teenage young ladies were required to spend two hours re-staining a small 25-foot-long wooden bridge over Mountain Creek in Macungie. A Monitor was present. She noted the time of start, and in exactly two hours she told her charges they could leave. I was annoyed at hearing that from one of the participants, because when I went to check on the work, it was plain to see that an extra ten minutes would have finished the job.

When serious misconduct needed adjudication, the punishment became enhanced. Shoplifting, stealing bicycles, setting fires, carrying guns and knives, breaking into homes were the behaviors that called for and received the strictest punishment. A long or short past history of delinquency was also a factor. The ultimate fate was a commitment to a juvenile detention facility. It appeared to me that too often placement provided an environment in which the juvenile learned even worse conduct. However, there were times when society needed to be protected. For less serious cases, we had available a facility named the Wiley House, now KidsPeace. Psychological evaluations were a tool in any placement. All such placements were required to be reviewed regularly.

Juvenile Court work had the advantage of not requiring the writing of opinions. At least I never recall writing one. For a whole day, I took on a long string of delinquency or adjudication cases, one at a time, until the list was complete. I might or might not ever see the same children again. I never knew how well the juvenile turned out.

# GOTTHARDT VS. MOLLOY

Moving away from my work in the Family Court Division (perhaps to return), I want briefly to take you over to the civil side of the system to demonstrate the shift in outlook that is needed by a judge when dealing with differing types of lawsuits. In Family Court, the judge cannot help but become deeply involved in the personal lives of persons who are often desperate for relief. In civil disputes, such as the up-coming Gotthardt case, a judge can be a little more dispassionate. The facts and law can prevail in an orderly and respectful proceeding. Civil Court cases are important, but they are not concerned with issues of how a mother is going to be able to feed her child.

The Gotthardt/Molloy negligence dispute that follows is included to give you a sense of the detail to which an appellate court reviews lower court judges. No judge wants to make a mistake. The consequence of a new trial with the delay that entails is more than unpleasant. I tried hard to make sound trial rulings and final decisions, but was well aware, in a positive manner, that if I made an error that hurt a litigant, there was a court that could and would correct the situation. The appellate judges are not subject to the time pressures of a trial court judge who must make a ruling during an ongoing trial. For a different perspective, I am presenting not my opinion or footnote, but instead, the Memorandum handed down by the appellate Superior Court.

J. 44043/89

```
RICHARD J. GOTTHARDT,           :    IN THE SUPERIOR COURT OF
                Appellant       :       PENNSYLVANIA
                                :
                                :
          v.                    :
                                :
                                :
CHRISTOPHER E. MOLLOY           :    No. 03552 Philadelphia 1988
```

Appeal from the Order Entered November 25, 1988
in the Court of Common Pleas of Lehigh County,
Civil No. 84-C-2223.

BEFORE:  CIRILLO, P.J., and ROWLEY and HESTER, JJ.

MEMORANDUM:                        **FILED** AUG 1 5 1989

This is an appeal from an order of the Court of Common
Pleas of Lehigh County which denied appellant Richard J.
Gotthardt's motion for a new trial following a jury verdict in
favor of appellee, Christopher Molloy. We affirm.

This civil action arose from a motor vehicle/pedestrian
accident which occurred on December 30, 1982, at the intersection
of Nineteenth and Tilghman Streets in Allentown, Pennsylvania. At
approximately 10:00 p.m. that evening, appellant, Richard
Gotthardt, a fifteen year-old high school student, attempted to
cross Tilghman Street in a northerly direction with a group of
friends. After venturing two-thirds of the way across Tilghman
Street, Gotthardt suddenly "dropped down low" as if he was
"clowning around," and doubled back towards the sidewalk where he
started. After two running strides in a southerly direction,
Gotthardt was struck by Christopher Molloy's vehicle, which was
proceeding in an easterly direction on Tilghman Street. Gotthardt
sustained various injuries as a result of the collision.

J. 44043/89 - 2

On December 13, 1984, Gotthardt commenced a civil action against Molloy, alleging negligence in the operation of his motor vehicle. Following discovery in the matter, a jury trial was held before the Honorable Robert K. Young in the Court of Common Pleas of Lehigh County. On January 14, 1987, the jury returned a verdict for Molloy, unanimously finding that Molloy committed no negligence in the operation of his vehicle. On January 16, 1987, Gotthardt filed a motion for a new trial, which was denied by Judge Young in an order dated October 27, 1988. This appeal followed.

Gotthardt advances the following three issues for our review:

I. Whether or not plaintiff is entitled to a new trial where the trial court conducted the trial before the jury with the conceptual framework that was exactly opposite of reality in that: 1) the jury was told that plaintiff may have ingested alcoholic beverages; and 2) the jury was not told that defendant admitted drinking alcoholic beverages prior to the accident, admitted drinking alcoholic beverages while actually operating the motor vehicle and the defendant affirmatively participated in a plan to hide the evidence of alcohol consumption from the police in order to avoid a breathalyzer?

II. Whether or not plaintiff is entitled to a new trial where the trial court denied plaintiff his rights to due process of law and a fair trial by affirmatively precluding the plaintiff from using at trial the deposition of an eyewitness who was unavailable to testify at trial, which deponent testified to facts which created a reasonable inference that defendant was intoxicated at the time of defendant's collision with plaintiff?

III. Whether or not plaintiff is entitled to a new trial where the trial court permitted defendant to elicit hearsay information from a

J. 44043/89 - 3

police officer concerning defendant's prior
consistent statements to the police?

Gotthardt's first issue for our review involves two
separate allegations of error. First, he claims that Judge Young
erred in granting Molloy's motion in limine which precluded
Gotthardt from introducing evidence that Molloy consumed alcoholic
beverages prior to the accident and while he was operating his
vehicle. Secondly, he maintains that a mistrial should have been
granted after defense counsel elicited, on cross-examination, a
comment from Gotthardt's companion Scott Sweeney which indicated
that Gotthardt may have ingested alcoholic beverages prior to
being hit at the intersection. We address each claim seriatim.

It is well-established in Pennsylvania that the
admission or exclusion of evidence which may be irrelevant,
confusing, misleading, cumulative or prejudicial is vested within
the sound discretion of the trial court, whose decision will not
be disturbed absent a clear abuse of that discretion. Concorde
Investments Inc. v. Gallagher, 345 Pa. Super. 49, 56, 497 A.2d
637, 641 (1985). Through his motion in limine, Molloy sought to
prevent all parties and counsel from making reference to his
ingestion of alcoholic beverages prior to the accident, or to the
presence of alcoholic beverages in his car at the time of the
accident. At the hearing on the motion, defense counsel Charles
Fonzone argued to Judge Young that evidence of drinking without
evidence of intoxication is inadmissible and its admission would
unduly prejudice his client. Attorney Fonzone stated:

> There is no witness who is going to testify
> that he was intoxicated. There is no
> Breathalyzer reading. There is no testimony

J. 44043/89 - 4

>   that the operation of his vehicle was erratic
>   or in any other manner other that the type of
>   driving required by the laws of Pennsylvania.
>   . . . You have no proof of intoxication here.
>   The mere fact of consuming alcohol is not
>   admissible in a civil action unless it
>   reasonably establishes intoxication. . . .
>   [T]he probative value of the evidence [of
>   alcohol consumption] is not such that it would
>   outweigh the prejudicial effect [to my
>   client].

Attorney Fonzone's representations of the law were correct.  In

<u>McKee by McKee v. Evans</u>, ___ Pa. Super. ___, 551 A.2d 260 (1988)

(en banc), we stated:

>   Since <u>Critzer v. Donovan</u>, 289 Pa. 381, 137 A.
>   665 (1927), it has been the rule in this
>   Commonwealth that when recklessness or
>   carelessness is at issue, proof of
>   intoxication is relevant, but the mere fact of
>   consuming alcohol is not admissible as being
>   unfairly prejudicial unless it reasonably
>   establishes intoxication.

___ Pa. Super. at ___, 551 A.2d at 281 (citation omitted).  Here,

the evidence elicited through deposition testimony, and at the <u>in</u>

<u>limine</u> hearing fell far short of that required to establish the

requisite degree of intoxication.  Molloy's testimony at

deposition indicated that he had consumed two beers in the span of

approximately two hours, and that there was an open bottle of beer

between his legs while he was driving.  The deposition testimony

of Wayne Simock, Molloy's passenger, corroborated Molloy's

testimony.  Clearly, Judge Young was not faced with sufficient

testimony which would reasonably establish a degree of

intoxication which proved Molloy's unfitness to drive.

Accordingly, we find that he committed no abuse of discretion in

granting Molloy's motion <u>in</u> <u>limine</u>.

J. 44043/89 - 5

Gotthardt next claims that a mistrial should have been granted where defense counsel elicited a comment from Scott Sweeney, Gotthardt's witness, which indicated that Gotthardt and his companions may have been drinking prior to crossing Tilghman Street.  During cross-examination of Scott Sweeney, the following testimony was elicited:

> ATTORNEY FONZONE:  Where had you been prior to being at the pizza shop at 19th and Allen?
>
> SCOTT SWEENEY:  What do you mean prior to the pizza shop?  Where we came from before that?
>
> ATTORNEY FONZONE:  Right.  Prior means before. Where were you before you were at the pizza shop?
>
> SCOTT SWEENEY:  All right.  There were six of us I think.  There is Billi, Kathy, John, Rick, myself, and Steve might have been there also.  We were standing by the 19th Street Theater and we had two beers split between six people.  Now, I didn't actually see Rick drink any, but I assume that he did since he was there.  I can't say how much he drank and I can't say how little he drank.

Attorney Orloski immediately motioned for a mistrial which was denied.  Judge Young did, however, issue a curative instruction to the jury.  Judge Young told the jurors:

> First of all, we had a little sidebar conference.  I can't tell you what we're doing, but in this case what happened was there was a mention of some beer here.  And you are going to hear all kinds of evidence, and sometimes the Judge has to tell you to do it.  It's not impossible, but it's difficult, but I'm going to direct you to do this, the fact that these boys had a few beers, if they did have them, is to be ignored by you and forgotten unless we have further evidence that there was some intoxication, that is, the fact that someone had beer.  In Pennsylvania anybody can have beer.  It may not affect you and your ability to[,] in this case[,] cross the street.  So at the moment[,] that

J. 44043/89 - 6

> discussion of beer is absolutely irrelevant
> and has nothing to do with the case and you
> are to ignore it. At the end of the trial we
> will see if anything further comes forward. I
> do not believe it will come forward, so he
> might as well had a glass of milk as far as
> you are concerned because beer itself in this
> situation is not illegal and it only becomes
> relevant if that beer is shown to have
> affected the conduct of the person who took
> it.

Our review of the notes of testimony immediately prior to Scott Sweeney's statement, the sidebar conference with Judge Young, and the curative instruction issued by the learned trial judge leads us to conclude that Judge Young committed no error in refusing to grant Gotthardt's motion for a mistrial. As the trial court aptly noted, attorney Fonzone's line of questioning was certainly not designed to elicit the statement that the group may have been consuming alcohol. Rather, it appears that he was merely testing Scott Sweeney's recollection of the events that evening, particularly since Sweeney's testimony deviated from his prior deposition statement that he did not remember where they had been prior to the accident. We also agree with the trial court's assessment that attorney Orloski must shoulder much of the responsibility for the witness's comment. Judge Young opined:

> There was never any [motion in limine] made on
> behalf of the plaintiff. Mr. Sweeney was
> plaintiff's witness. Mr. Sweeney had been
> deposed by both attorneys prior to trial.
> During that deposition, Mr. Sweeney mentioned
> the possibility that plaintiff had consumed
> alcoholic beverages. Therefore, since counsel
> for the plaintiff had prior knowledge about
> plaintiff's alcohol consumption, he could also
> have made a motion In Limine. Furthermore,
> even if plaintiff's counsel felt a motion In
> Limine was unnecessary, proper witness
> preparation would have prevented Mr. Sweeney's
> alleged damaging statement.

J. 44043/89 - 7

In light of the inculpable manner in which the witness's statement was elicited, and the prompt curative instruction that immediately followed, we cannot conclude that the fleeting mention of alcohol consumption was so highly prejudicial as to warrant the award of a new trial. We therefore dismiss this allegation of error as meritless.

As an adjunct to his first issue, Gotthardt also maintains that attorney Fonzone drew the jury's attention to his alleged alcohol consumption by questioning his treating physician about the absence of blood work tests in the medical records. This question, he maintains, inferred that there was medical evidence of alcohol consumption in the hospital record, and that Gotthardt attempted to conceal it by removing it from the charts. We cannot agree.

Dr. Suggs deposition testimony, which was read to the jury at trial, reveals the following passage:

> ATTORNEY FONZONE: Dr. Suggs, you have what's before you, I believe marked Plaintiff's Exhibit No. 2, and as you look through that, you indicated there was indication of blood work in there. Does that hospital record that you have as Plaintiff's No. 2 have any blood test results?
>
> DR. SUGGS: No, it does not.
>
> ATTORNEY FONZONE: Is that unusual?
>
> DR. SUGGS: Blood test results are certainly part of his hospital chart. I have no knowledge of why there are not part of this photocopy.
>
> ATTORNEY FONZONE: So they should be there then, is that a -- if this were a complete copy of the chart.

J. 44043/89 - 8

DR. SUGGS:   For completeness I would suspect
so.

We fail to see how this brief reference to the absence of
medically necessary blood test results aroused the inference of
alcohol consumption, or in any way emphasized the fact that
Gotthardt may have been drinking prior to the accident.  Attorney
Fonzone's line of questioning focused on routine blood test
results, and <u>not</u> blood-alcohol test results.  Moreover, because of
the absence of the blood test results in his copy of the hospital
records, attorney Fonzone was merely following up on Dr. Suggs
testimony on direct examination that "[Gotthardt had] routine
laboratory studies done, routine blood testing, which were all
within normal limits . . . ."  Because this innocuous line of
questioning does not in any way infer, as Gotthardt suggests, the
presence of medical evidence of intoxication, or that Gotthardt
was somehow "hiding evidence of intoxication," we find that Judge
Young committed no abuse of discretion in permitting the passage
to be read to the jury.

Gotthardt next claims that the trial court erred in
precluding him from using at trial the deposition testimony of
Wayne Simock, a passenger in Molloy's vehicle, who was unavailable
to testify at trial.  Gotthardt maintains that Pennsylvania Rule
of Civil Procedure 4020 authorized the use of the deposition, and
Judge Young committed reversible error in omitting it from
evidence.  We cannot agree.

Rule 4020 provides, in pertinent part:

(a) At the trial, any part or all of a
deposition, <u>so far as admissible under the
rules of evidence</u>, may be used against any

J. 44043/89 - 9

> party who was present or represented at the
> taking of the deposition or who had notice
> thereof if required, in accordance with any
> one of the following provisions:
>
> (3)The deposition of a witness, whether or not
> a party, may be used by any party for any
> purpose if the court finds

* * *

>> (b) that the witness is at a greater
>> distance than one hundred (100)
>> miles from the place of trial or is
>> outside the Commonwealth, unless it
>> appears that the absence of the
>> witness was procured by the party
>> offering the deposition, . . .

Pa.R.C.P. 4020(a)(3)(b) (emphasis added). While there is no dispute that Wayne Simock was unavailable for trial pursuant to Rule 4020(a)(3)(b) because of his duties in the United States Army, that does not necessarily mean, as Gotthardt suggests, that his deposition testimony was "admissible under the rules of evidence." Wayne Simock's deposition was taken at the offices of attorney Fonzone, and it was Fonzone's associate who conducted the direct examination of Simock. Attorney Orloski then questioned Simock, as on cross-examination, utilizing leading and suggestive questions. At trial, Gotthardt sought to read the cross-examination of Wayne Simock to the jurors. In effect, Gotthardt attempted to call Simock as his own witness, and then cross-examine him. The propriety of this exact scenario was addressed by this court in Pascone v. Thomas Jefferson University, 357 Pa. Super. 524, 516 A.2d 384 (1986), alloc. granted 531 A.2d 431 (1986), appeal dismissed 536 A.2d 338 (1987). There, we stated:

> "[I]t has long been held that one may not lead
> his own witnesses with suggestive questions."
> The limitation on the form of questions which

J. 44043/89 - 10

> a party may ask his own witness is not
> modified by Pa.R.C.P. 4020(d) which permits
> the introduction of deposition testimony by
> either party. "The distinction, applicable to
> live witnesses called to the stand, between
> the direct examination form of questioning and
> the cross-examination form of questioning,
> remains fully applicable." In the instant
> case, although plaintiffs wanted the jury to
> hear their cross-examination of Dr. Smith,
> they were making him their own witness when
> they offered into evidence his deposition
> testimony. As the Pascones' witness, Dr.
> Smith could not testify by way of leading
> questions asked by plaintiff's counsel. This
> is true just as if the doctor's testimony had
> been given from the witness stand in open
> court. . . . [Additionally,] Dr. Smith cannot
> be characterized as a hostile witness . . . .

357 Pa. Super. at 531-32, 516 A.2d at 388 (citations omitted).
Faced with a factual scenario closely akin to Pascone, and the
absence of any indication that Wayne Simock was a hostile witness
to Gotthardt, Judge Young properly determined that Gotthardt was
not entitled to read Wayne Simock's deposition testimony into
evidence. We therefore dismiss this claim as specious.

Lastly, Gotthardt claims that he is entitled to a new
trial because Judge Young permitted Molloy to elicit testimony
from Officer Robert Webre, the investigating officer, regarding
Molloy's statements following the accident. Gotthardt claims that
"[t]he statement elicited was a self-serving statement which
Defendant made to the police officer sometime during the officer's
investigation after arrival at the scene."

We note, however, that it was Gotthardt's attorney who
opened the door for admission of this testimony. While Judge
Young had directed defense counsel not to ask the officer about
any statements by Molloy immediately following the accident, it

J. 44043/89 - 11

was attorney Orloski, on cross-examination, who asked the officer "What did Molloy tell you [about] how fast he was going?" In effect, attorney Orloski waived the trial court's ruling concerning the officer's testimony by pursuing that line of questioning. We therefore agree with Judge Young's cogent observation that "[i]t would be improper for the court to let plaintiff's counsel now hide behind the shield of protection that he discarded." We therefore dismiss this final claim as meritless.

Based on the forgoing, we conclude that Judge Young committed no clear or palpable abuse of discretion in denying Gotthardt's motion for a new trial, see Stevenson v. General Motors Corp., 513 Pa. 411, 521 A.2d 413 (1987), and we therefore affirm his order.

Order affirmed.

# THE PRIVATE NATURE OF JUDGING

I have heard it said that judging is a lonely job. There is some truth to that idea. When you are given a lawsuit to decide, you must not ask any other judges or people what they think you ought to do regarding factual or legal issues. You have heard the witnesses and determined their credibility. You and the lawyers have debated together about the proper statutes and precedents to be applied. It would not be fair to them or their clients for you to listen to an outsider who had not been sworn in or cross-examined. So, in essence, the judge is alone with his cases.

There are times, however, when it might be helpful to get some advice about issues of procedure. For example, how many alternate jurors in a complicated medical malpractice case are needed; where is the restaurant that will most promptly deliver to the courthouse to feed the jury; and what is the safest way of getting a prisoner into the courtroom.

A judge is also cut off from the public in other situations. A judge is not permitted to sit on the Boards of Directors of Banks, Insurance Companies, Non-profit Organizations and any entities that may likely come before his or her court.

Appellate judges sit together and, of course, debate the issues among each other. Not so in the trial courts. It would be a serious error for any judge to give advice to a trial judge in an ongoing matter. This brings me to the story my colleague, James N. Diefenderfer told me in his chambers. He was very upset, he said, because he had just been advised by Pennsylvania's then Chief Justice, R. N., to allow in certain evidence that Judge Diefenderfer had already ruled was not admissible in a pending trial. Counsel for the party that had failed to prevail in Diefenderfer's ruling had somehow reached the Chief Justice and persuaded him to intervene. Diefenderfer reversed his decision and permitted the disputed evidence. A Complaint to the Judicial Conduct Board was filed, I was told, and was in the process of being investigated when the Chief Justice died.

One last story about getting advice from fellow judges. At some sort of judges' get-together, probably lunch, we were discussing the fine quality of our trial bar, seriously. One of my bench-mates agreed as to the skill of Lawyer X, but advised the rest of us, "when he looks at you and his eyebrows go way up, he's probably lying."

The "eyebrow" comment created a laugh, but such a generalization should be of little value to a trial judge. The individual clients of each attorney are entitled to be heard "de novo," that is, with a clean slate. Whether or not you like or trust a person's lawyer is irrelevant. The object is to uncover the truth from all sources. No counsel should be able to fool you on matters of the law. The facts of a case seldom come from just the attorney, and can be verified or disbelieved the same as any party or witness. No prejudging.

# A Judge's Staff: Court Crier, Secretary, Law Clerk, Deputy Sheriff, Tipstaff

I may have been alone on the bench, but my new job came with what is called a "staff." That is, some helpful and talented people who are essential to the goal of maximum productivity. I have typed this book before taking it to a publisher, but without my judicial secretary typing my opinions and letters and answering the telephone, hardly anything could be accomplished.

I was allowed to choose a Court Crier. Someone not only to open court, but who had the responsibility of keeping the cases coming; to call or find the lawyers who were up for the next case, or let them know how the schedule for the day was progressing. The Court Crier also was in charge of seeing that I had the needed files which I tried to review before the case started.

The Court Crier sometimes needed help in order to keep the cases moving along in what was a judicial assembly line. The helper was called a tipstaff. An old English word for "gofer." When we were in a jury trial, the tipstaff organized the bathroom trips, and took files, orders, and opinions back to the proper courthouse office. He (my tipstaff was a he – my Court Crier a she) kept the water pitchers full and in general covered those items that the Court Crier could not attend to when court was busy.

My secretary, Barbara Yost, worked for me for a total of thirty-four years, including the eleven and a half years that I was a judge. She was really in charge of the staff. She could not only read and type my handwritten opinions, she could spell! I never could. If it was not for the spell-check feature of my old Gateway word processor, this book to you would have taken twice as long. I can use a dictionary, but it slows the work down when I have to have a pretty good idea how to spell a word before it can be tracked down to a certainty.

Barbara also answered the telephone if I was not in the office. If I was in the office, I answered it because almost all of the calls were for me. I had to stop myself from calling other lawyers and asking their secretaries to tell their boss that Bob Young had called. The secretaries were being reprimanded for not giving Judge Young priority. On an average day, I arrived at about 7:30 in the morning. I then had at least an hour of quiet time to work on whatever was on the top of the pile, preparing for about an hour's dictation to Barbara on her "steno pad". My commute took 22 minutes; she had a drive from the little Borough of Bally on a congested State route that took her at least 45 minutes.

Another staff-member was a law clerk. Law clerks came to learn, and yet I was the one who learned the most from them. Having young people around is mentally stimulating. Fresh out of law school they have new ideas and are up to date on the changing laws. They know how to research. They still have enthusiasm and humor. I suppose a trial judge could get along without one, but who would produce the spark of fun?

Not officially on a judge's staff, is a deputy sheriff. Now here is a key person. In Lehigh County, the sheriff himself is in charge of courthouse security, among other duties. He assigns a deputy to each courtroom. With a few exceptions, I was assigned the same deputy all of the time. For the first four or five years, it was Rudy Black, who moved on to manage a drug store. For the balance of my term, my deputy was Charles Farmer. He has died. Having a uniformed sheriff in my courtroom when sitting was essential. Both of these men somehow knew just when they should move up toward the bench, or stay back. Our State has seen several judges shot on the bench. Criminal Trials, Hearings, Guilty Pleas, Support Court, Custody disputes all generate tension and anger.

I received a shooting threat only once. Not arising out of a case in the Criminal or Family Courts, but tied to an estate matter in Orphans' Court. A mother and son had lived together for many years. When the mother died, the home and other items needed to be distributed to the son and his sister (his mother's daughter). The son did not have the money to buy out his sister. He refused to leave the home. I issued an Order of eviction. The Emmaus police informed the County Sheriff that the son was known to be armed, and that he had threatened me. My assigned deputy sheriff asked for instructions. I told him to bring the son into my office and stand by. After the son and I had about a half hour two-way discussion, I let him leave. In due course, his mother's estate was settled after he found new accommodations. I think I became a real person to him, not just some cold judge on a leather high back chair.

# JAN THWAITES AND BARBARA YOST

A nd then there was Jan Thwaites. She started as a law clerk with Judge Coyne. When he retired, I inherited her along with the responsibility for all of the Orphans' Court work. So, I really had two law clerks. At first, she primarily focused on overseeing the audit of the accounts of decedents' estates and trusts. I did not consult with her about the other cases in that division. I wanted it understood that there would be no continuation of Judge Coyne's reign, and that I would take charge. It did not take too long to discover that Jan had a great deal more to offer both myself and the court. Together we were able to keep current and take on some matters of importance to the litigants and the community. Jan and I, and Barbara, continue our friendships, irregularly meeting for lunch or breakfast.

*Sharon K. Merkel of Images.*
**To the left Jan Thwaites, to the right, Barbara Yost.**

# CHOOSING LAW CLERKS

I discussed the real value of law clerks. I think you might enjoy the way they came to me. I use that phrase because although I had a series of eight, I only picked one. I was confirmed by the Senate in early spring of 1984. I needed time to finish some pending work and then shovel the rest of the cases to my son/partner Donald. Knowing that the law schools would be graduating a class soon, I started looking for a law clerk well before being sworn in, in June. I called the Penn Law School placement department and asked if there were any prospects I could interview. Whoever I spoke with did not think so. I was a little late in making that request, and perhaps their seniors had already found employment.

I made the same call to the Dickinson Law School. The woman on the other line said she was sure that several applicants would appreciate being considered. I asked her to corral four or five, and set a date to visit the school. Carolyn and I drove to Carlisle one afternoon and went through the process of asking and being asked about wide-ranging personal experiences. All of the almost-lawyers presented themselves well. It was a pleasant afternoon, but we did not learn about such things as their individual study habits, writing ability or recreational choices. Nevertheless, we settled upon a cheerful bow-tied young gentleman by the name of Christopher Gittinger (Chris).

It was an excellent choice, but I knew that we had been lucky. At the end of Chris's two years as my in-house squire, I asked him to go out to his alma mater and choose his replacement. I explained that he could move around in the school and learn about the habits, personality, class standing and other attributes that he believed would be most useful as a law clerk. He agreed, and thereafter all of my clerks picked their successor. It worked for me.

# SWEARING IN JURORS

In an effort to make the jurors aware of the importance of the function that they were performing for the whole community, I had my Court Crier bring the courtroom to rise when the jury entered. My colleagues and I shared in producing a short film for the purpose of orienting our jurors. It was shown to the entire jury panel before the clerk began a random call of individuals who were then assigned to a particular case. The lawyers narrowed down the final case list of twelve jurors. The Judge was only called to rule upon the qualifications of a juror if there was a disagreement between the attorneys. I found that although very few persons wanted to be a juror, once they were seated and realized the importance of the job, most jurors later stated that they valued the experience.

We had excellent clerical staff in the courtroom. Depending upon under which division we were operating, the clerks kept giving and taking from me the files on an "as needed" basis. When I started judging, the Oath to tell the truth was administered to each witness by a clerk. At this, clerks were terrible. They had done it so many times, that no sense of importance was left at the speed delivered. I took over that job. I believe it was a bit more sobering for the judge to look at you and ask you to swear or affirm to the truth, rather than a busy young clerk. In the 1950's, when I served as a volunteer Public Defender, the Court Reporters administrated the oath to witnesses. Joe Gallagher and Nellie Sweiffel were the two I remember. I think the Bible was still being used, but I recall the words that admonished the telling of the truth "...so help you God as you shall answer on the last great day." My little effort merely asked: Do you swear or affirm to tell the truth in this matter?

# COURT REPORTERS

O ur Court of Common Pleas is known as a "Court of Record." Transcripts of all court proceedings are available, if needed, at a reasonable cost. The court reporters sat quite near the witness chair, and when I was judging, they no longer "took shorthand." They used a finger-manipulated device that produced connected pieces of paper with markings that could be transcribed into typed words. The court reporters were exceptionally skilled, which showed when they were handling a medical malpractice case and had to repeat aloud medical terms.

There was then a "pool" of court reporters who were assigned to various judges at different times depending on what a judge was doing. They were not needed, for example, for Argument Court, or settlement conferences or other matters that had no chance of being appealed. It was mostly the appellate courts that required a verbatim record in their review of our lower court decisions. Not ever knowing who might need a record of what was being said—except with two exceptions I will tell you about later—I do not believe I ever started court without a court reporter present. There was nobody more important. Our system abhors secrecy, and open and transparent courts are essential in a democracy.

# NO GAVEL, NO RAISING FUNDS

I need to dispel a perception that I am sure my Great-Grandchildren have no doubt picked up from watching too many old TV movies. You are probably watching the ones I have seen and am seeing again. In those shows, the judge, a tyrant or an alcoholic, is perpetually banging his gavel in order to quell a courtroom disturbance. I am sorry to report, that your antecedent judge has never even had a gavel with him on the bench. The presence of a judge and a deputy Sheriff kept things quiet enough. My crier did, however, open the Court with those magic words O' Yez, O' Yez, O' Yez, and then he would bang the gavel that he had.

A condition of becoming a judge is the rule that prohibits raising money for charity, any charity. It is difficult to explain that restriction when being asked by some very reputable organizations to help solicit funds for their programs. The reason for the policy is that litigants or prospective litigants will attempt to favorably influence a judge's opinion of them if they give large sums to the judge's pet charity when he asks for a donation. Judges are not even allowed to be listed as officers of a charity on its solicitation letters.

The chief executive of the Minsi Trails Council of the Boy Scouts of America apparently did not know that. To my surprise and chagrin, he listed me with the other members of the executive committee on a fund drive letter. I immediately reported this to a member of the State's Judicial Ethics Committee (Judge Edward D. Reibman), who, although unhappy, did not suggest a reprimand or retraction by the Scout Council under the circumstances. I should not have assumed the Director's awareness.

Of course, judges can give anonymously. And, judges can take part in Bar Association sponsored programs such as "Lawyers Helping Lawyers," which provides training for the purpose of aiding addicted or alcoholic lawyers. Judge Carol K. McGinley and I joined that effort, traveling to Wernersville, Berks County.

I understand the rule, but it does remove you from the kinds of people with whom more contact would be a benefit.

# KEEPING SILENT

Another prohibition attached to a judgeship requires that at every judicial level the officeholder or candidate is not permitted to say what he or she may or may not believe about any topic of discussion that might conceivably come before the court. The rule is completely understandable, by the judges, but I have observed that some of the public are unhappy with being unable to find out what a judicial candidate or sitting judge thinks about a specific social issue. Although our free speech rights are thus limited, the policy balances the need for us to provide due process impartiality.

One way of keeping in touch with real people was to perform marriages. We were not permitted to accept a fee, although one local judge told me how happy he was to perform a wedding where he was asked to join the party after the ceremony for a first-class meal in a very fancy hotel. Even after retirement ex-judges who served a full 10-year term remain able to perform marriages. At the several dozen weddings that I performed over the period I was a judge, if they were in my courtroom, I directed the bride and groom to step up into an area where the clerks sat during court, and to turn facing the witnesses and guests so that everyone could see them. I remained on the lower level with my back to the audience. Why any couple wants its guests to see the back of their heads during a wedding is a mystery to me.

# THE SEMI-ANNUAL JUDICIAL CONFERENCES AND THE NATIONAL JUDICIAL COLLEGE

Every year while I was a judge, the State's Office of Judicial Administration held semi-annual educational conferences. In the summer, almost all of the trial judges met at the Hershey Hotel, and the winter meetings alternated between Philadelphia and Pittsburgh. They were a bit lavish, but the lesson sessions were valuable. It was encouraging to learn about the problems and solutions that other judges discussed. Carolyn was allowed to attend those meetings, upon payment by us of most of her expenses. Some nice side trips were arranged for our spouses.

About a year after I began my new job, I followed the advice of someone now forgotten, and enrolled in the National Judicial College, a school specifically created for the purpose of training trial judges. It is located in Reno, Nevada, within the campus of the University of Nevada. Carolyn and I stayed in the College Inn, across the street from the fair sized single floor facility. The College Inn was a good choice of lodging. It was within walking distance of Downtown, where the well-known arching sign across the main street proclaims Reno to be the "Biggest Little City in America." By chance, we arrived just in time to see the famous Reno Air Show.

I chose to take the three-week General Jurisdiction course. There were approximately twenty-five other State judges in my "class." They came from all sections of the country. Participants were encouraged to share our divergent local practices and were challenged to improve them. Toward the end of the program the mantra evolved into chants of "Give them a Hearing!" Looking back, I believe that the Reno experience was well worth the effort and very rewarding. Speaking of being rewarding, Carolyn and I had free time after 4:00 p. m. and normally took the sidewalks to the downtown for inexpensive food and a little bit of 25 Cent slot machine play. Our limit was $20.00. Carolyn learned how to read the bar code on the free prize coupons. We went home with a lot of little pens and playing cards, and a new friend from Cobb County, Georgia, Rusty Carlisle with whom we still correspond and occasionally visit.

We revisited The National Judicial College twice, not for more casino trinkets, but to attend one week-long study of Dispute Resolutions. I returned armed with materials and enthusiasm, and was able to convince the Court Administrator that our County should institute two new programs. With some mild resistance from the Family Law Bar, Mediation was required in divorce and property disposition cases, and several Masters were appointed to try to bring the parties together in custody of children matters. I understand that both programs are still in place, delivering satisfactory results.

The second one-week symposium focused on the use of scientific evidence in court. Our legal system prides itself on providing a predicable body of laws and judicial precedents. The people, and especially attorneys, need to be able to know the rules. They look to the past to learn what has been approved by prior courts in similar situations. When new technologies appear, the courts are slow to recognize their validity, and generally do not authorize their use by a jury or themselves until a substantial body of scholars have expressed an opinion about their reliability. The week was spent learning about such things as the nature and use of blood types, alcohol breathalyzers, eye scans, DNA and gun/bullet identification. Interesting, and I was able to put some of that knowledge to use in paternity and criminal cases.

# ST. LUKE'S "RIGHT TO DIE" CASE

Those who know me will tell you, and I will affirm, that while my head tried to understand the nature and importance of the many varieties of cases in the differing Divisions of the Court system, it was the work flowing out of the Orphans' Court that claimed my heart.

There was a "right-to-die" case that I will never forget. The Court's file is properly sealed, there was no appeal, and I have no copy of my final Decree. This is what I vividly recall.

I received a telephone call from counsel for St. Luke's Hospital in the early evening before I had left the courthouse. He told me that the hospital's doctors were treating an elderly bed-ridden man for serious medical conditions that they believed needed to be treated. However, the wife of the patient was at the hospital and refused to allow the doctors to proceed.

The doctors were not sure that the patient was fully able to understand the consequences of either treatment or lack of treatment. How, the attorney asked, could the man consent, and what authority did the wife have? Time was surely running out for the husband if nothing was done. Could I help?

I, of course, had to hesitate and think. I had no court reporter at hand, but I did have a working tape recorder. I asked the attorney if the doctors were at the hospital, and would they and he be there to testify if I came to the Fountain Hill facility at about 6:30 p. m. He was also to tell the wife that I was coming. He agreed, and I left for the "hearing" with pad, pen, and the old cassette tape recorder.

It had occurred to me during the telephone call and while driving to the hospital that the wife might have a financial or other interest in the death of her husband. Why did she attempt to refuse him medical care?

The attorney met me at the hospital's entrance and we, with the doctors, gathered somewhere in a hallway for a brief conference. They explained in medical terms the nature of the man's condition and said that without chemotherapy the husband would die. They were not able to predict how long he would live if they aggressively treated him. I asked the doctors to wait for me in the cafeteria.

I asked to see his wife. She was in her husband's hospital room. When I entered she quietly stood with me as I asked a few questions about their ages and how long they had been married. I told her the essence of what the doctors had told me. She said she understood, but began to cry, telling me that he should not have to undergo any more pain. Our conversation was muted, but the husband must have heard enough of it that he raised his head a little and asked and motioned me to come over to the side of his bed. I did so, and asked him if he understood what would happen if he refused further medical help. He did not answer the question directly, but feebly held up one arm at a time so that I could see the dark blue under-the-skin patches, all over both arms, and weakly said at least three or more times, "Let me go."

All I can remember saying, was "all right." I met the doctors, and told them that I found that their patient was competent for the purpose of giving his consent to deny further treatment, and that I would issue such an order the next morning. I never did turn on the tape recorder.

# ELECTRIC SHOCK TREATMENTS

The first time that an attorney presented a Petition to Permit Electric Shock Treatment in Orphans' Court Motion Court, I had no idea that it was my lot to decide such a matter. The lawyer showed me the relevant statute or regulation. I did not have a clue as to the need or effect for shock treatment, although it sounded pretty extreme. I told the attorney that I needed to talk to the doctor and see the procedure. I believe that it was that day or the next day in the evening on the way home that I visited the hospital. You will be happy to know that the sedated patient exhibited no violent jerks or cries of pain, although some mild twitching was visible. The doctor explained more than I wanted to know, but did convince me that the treatment would do no harm and had a reasonable chance of slowly, with several treatments, bringing her back from her debilitating depression. I signed the Order for Treatment, and a few more Orders over the years for other patients.

The Orphans' Court jurisdiction also required me to oversee any settlements that were due to a minor. Most of these arose out of motor vehicle accident, medical malpractice, or product liability cases. I first needed to decide if the sum being offered was reasonable under the circumstances of the particular case being settled. I reviewed the attorney's fees. Knowing that the child could not be given the funds directly, I asked for suggestions. That discussion always led to a complete study of the child's history and future needs. His or her parents or guardian were present which gave me a fairly accurate idea of what the minor was facing in the long run. Depending upon factors such as age, any disabilities and educational goals, I most often favored a structured settlement, placed through an insurance company. The process was not as tedious as it might seem. Here was a child whom I could protect and assure that this once in a lifetime fund of money would be only for its benefit.

A significant amount of time was used by Jan Thwaites and a special Estate Auditor to review the Accounts filed by fiduciaries such as Trustees and Executors. Judge Coyne had established a thorough system requiring an explanation in detail of the handling of assets and expenditures. Again, the task was for the purpose of protecting the wishes of the decedent or settlor. The Court needed to be assured that all of the inheritance taxes, debts and proper fees had been paid, and that the beneficiaries had received their proper shares. As the Administrative Judge of the Orphans' Court responsibility for those duties devolved upon me. The work was far from routine.

During my time at that job, there were excellent relationships between the local Banks, Trust Companies, the Court, and members of the Bar. If there were problems, those were normally worked out before the Estate or Trust Accounts were called before the Court for Audit. There were times when it became necessary to reduce trustee or legal fees, or surcharge a fiduciary for an improper charge. Working with a committee of lawyers who did most of the estate work, a Fee Memorandum was developed, as a guide, which I have been told is still being applied. A copy of the Fee Memorandum is included in the Internet site www.trialjudgebook.com.

To give you an idea of the kinds of issues that occurred in the audit process, I recall my disbelief when I saw an executor son charge his father's estate for the cost of attending his father's funeral. I disallowed that charge. In another estate, I removed an executrix because she acknowledged that she had withheld the distribution of her father's assets to herself and the other beneficiaries to avoid sharing her bequest with her estranged husband. She had planned to wait until her divorce was final.

# N.E.S. "RIGHT TO DIE" CASE

For more than six years N. E. S. had been confined to a bed in the Lehigh County Nursing Home at Cedarbrook. She had been placed there following a fall from which she suffered a massive brain injury. She had not spoken or performed any of the daily activities of life since her injury.

I received a Petition from her parents seeking permission to end her life by withdrawing vital medical procedures. The Commonwealth's Attorney General, the District Attorney, the County of Lehigh and the Lehigh Valley Hospital each had a keen interest in the matter. I appointed a Guardian ad Litem to represent N. E. S., and scheduled a date for a Hearing, which was to be held at the nursing home.

Counsel for all of the parties, the attending physicians, two of the attending nurses, a court reporter and myself met at her bedside. The law dictated that to permit her to expire I had to be clearly convinced that she would remain for the foreseeable future in a "persistent vegetative state." All during the Hearing I watched in turn as each of the people in the room tried to obtain any response from her. The nurses testified that they noticed moments of attention from her. The medical doctors could not agree as to whether or not she had a reasonable chance of slow improvement.

There was no urgency for a decision. She was in no danger. I did not believe that a quick Order was a good idea. I wanted to collect my thoughts, and I also wanted all of the parties to know that I recognized their individual positions. The feelings of the attending nurses were a factor. They had worked very hard to bring their patient back to a communicative life, and believed that their efforts were worthwhile. An immediate decision by me might, I thought, be depressing for the whole nursing staff. Further, this was not a case where a person refuses medical care. Here she was receiving the best care, and the request was to intentionally cause her death. My Decree and Opinion follow.

Trial Judge: A Job Description

IN THE COURT OF COMMON PLEAS OF LEHIGH COUNTY, PENNSYLVANIA

ORPHANS' COURT DIVISION

N.E.S., an Incompetent, by   )
H.R.S. and J.M.S., her   )
Guardians,   )
   )
       Petitioners   )
   )
       vs.   )
   )
THE COUNTY OF LEHIGH, DEPT.   )   No. 1987-418A
OF CEDARBROOK NURSING HOMES;   )
LEHIGH VALLEY HOSPITAL CENTER; )
ERNEST D. PREATE,JR., ESQ.,   )
ATTORNEY GENERAL FOR THE   )
COMMONWEALTH OF PENNSYLVANIA; )
and ROBERT L. STEINBERG, ESQ.,)
DISTRICT ATTORNEY FOR THE   )
COUNTY OF LEHIGH,   )
   )
       Respondents   )

**FINAL DECREE**

NOW, this 4th day of June, 1992, for the reasons contained in the attached Opinion, the Petitioners' request that they be authorized to discontinue all extraordinary procedures for sustaining the vital processes of N.E.S., including artificial nutrition and hydration tubes, is Denied.

BY THE COURT:

Robert K. Young, Judge

IN THE COURT OF COMMON PLEAS OF LEHIGH COUNTY, PENNSYLVANIA

ORPHANS' COURT DIVISION

| | |
|---|---|
| N.E.S., an Incompetent, by<br>H.R.S. and J.M.S., her<br>Guardians,<br><br>   Petitioners<br><br>   vs.<br><br>THE COUNTY OF LEHIGH, DEPT.<br>OF CEDARBROOK NURSING HOMES;<br>LEHIGH VALLEY HOSPITAL CENTER;<br>ERNEST D. PREATE, JR., ESQ.,<br>ATTORNEY GENERAL FOR THE<br>COMMONWEALTH OF PENNSYLVANIA;<br>and ROBERT L. STEINBERG, ESQ.,<br>DISTRICT ATTORNEY FOR THE<br>COUNTY OF LEHIGH,<br><br>   Respondents | No. 1987-418A |

* * * * *

APPEARANCES:

   MICHAEL J. PIOSA, ESQUIRE,
   And with him, WEAVER, MOSEBACH, PIOSA,
   HIXSON & MARLES,
    On behalf of the Petitioners.

   CATHARINE M. ROSEBERRY, ESQUIRE,
   ASSISTANT COUNTY SOLICITOR,
    On behalf of the County of Lehigh,
    Department of Cedarbrook Nursing Homes.

   MATTHEW SORRENTINO, ESQUIRE,
   And with him, TALLMAN, HUDDERS & SORRENTINO,
    On behalf of Lehigh Valley Hospital Center,
    now known as Lehigh Valley Hospital - I-78
    and Cedar Crest.

LINDA C. BARRETT, ESQUIRE,
DEPUTY ATTORNEY GENERAL, as <u>parens</u> <u>patriae</u>.

ROBERT L. STEINBERG, ESQUIRE, DISTRICT
ATTORNEY, and MARCIE MARINO, ESQUIRE,
ASSISTANT DISTRICT ATTORNEY,
    for the County of Lehigh.

FRANCES A. FRUHWIRTH, ESQUIRE,
And with her, FONZONE AND ASHLEY,
    As Guardian Ad Litem for N.E.S.


\*     \*     \*     \*     \*


## OPINION

ROBERT K. YOUNG, Judge.

It is to the mother and father of N.E.S. that this intentionally brief Opinion is written. The Court's words will be of little consolation, but I am obliged to state the reasons for the Decree just entered. The usual recitation of the facts is not needed, as no one knows better than you what has happened to your daughter.

Please understand that Trial Judges are restricted to the job of upholding the laws as set down by the people of this Commonwealth through either their elected Legislators or elected Appellate Courts. In order for me to grant your Petition, I would have to be clearly convinced that N.E.S. was living in a persistent vegetative state.

-2-

The very excellent medical specialists who testified could not agree on whether that fact was true. After having seen her, and after listening to what all of her caretakers say she is doing, I believe that her mind and body are able to respond to her environment in a rudimentary fashion. While she is clearly not the person she was before her massive brain injury, she has shown very slow and slight improvement in the almost six years since her fall. At the present time she is awake and, to a degree, aware of her surroundings.

Under the above facts, the law does not permit me to consider whether she would choose to continue to function as she is. It has become the public policy in Pennsylvania to differentiate between the rights of incompetents (soon to be called incapacitated persons) and the general public. A mentally alert citizen maintains a constitutionally protected right to refuse medical treatment. That so-called "right to die" is grounded upon principles of privacy and self-determination. When someone is incapacitated, however, it is only when their condition is "terminal", or when they are in a "state of permanent unconsciousness" that it becomes permissible to withhold or withdraw life-sustaining treatment.

-3-

53

I have offered the above explanation in an effort to relieve you from your terrible burden. You have done all that you can as the parents and guardians of your child in her present condition.

# THE ESTATE OF M. K.: A HOMELESS LADY FOUND TO BE INCAPACITATED

As is often said, the Orphans' Court helps those who cannot help themselves. It has jurisdiction over the incapacitated, minors, decedents' estates, individual and charitable trusts, non-profit corporations, and even cemeteries. Who else is going to make sure that what a person wants to happen at their death is faithfully carried out? The Orphans' Court Judge is the one who appoints guardians for minors and citizens who have forgotten how to perform the daily necessities of life. If non-profits lose their charitable nature, it is the Orphans' Court that should step in. When the trustees spend money inappropriately, that court can require surcharges and compel resignations.

The following M. K. case will help provide an understanding of the kind of problems the judge must consider in one particular incapacitation matter.

IN THE COURT OF COMMON PLEAS OF LEHIGH COUNTY, PENNSYLVANIA

ORPHANS' COURT DIVISION

In re:                )
)
   Estate of        )
                  )  No. 1994-0405
   M. K.,           )
)
   An Incapacitated Person  )

* * * * *

APPEARANCES:

     THOMAS C. ANEWALT, ESQUIRE,
     And with him, BLACK, McCARTHY, EIDELMAN,
       ANEWALT, KERCHER, P.C.
       On behalf of the Petitioner.

     HELEN Z. STAUFFER, ESQUIRE,
     And with her, FITZPATRICK, LENTZ & BUBBA, P.C.
       On behalf of the Incapacitated Person.

     GWIN M. KROUSE, ESQUIRE,
       Guardian Ad Litem for the Incapacitated Person.

* * * * *

OPINION

ROBERT K. YOUNG, Judge.

    Following three Hearings, held on May 4, 1994, June 1, 1994, and June 10, 1994, the Court decreed on June 13, 1994 that M.K. was an Incapacitated Person. Peter D. Johnstone, Executive Director of the Lehigh County Area

55

Agency on Aging, was appointed as the Limited Guardian of the Person and Estate of M.K. That Order has been appealed and thus this Opinion is necessary.

A Petition to Declare M.K. an Incapacitated Person was filed by the Lehigh County Area Agency on Aging (Agency) on April 4, 1994. On that same day, Helen Z. Stauffer, Esquire, was appointed as legal counsel for M.K. A Citation was issued and served, setting May 4, 1994 as the Hearing date. M.K. did not appear on that day, although her Counsel was present. Following the testimony, the Court appointed Peter Johnstone in his capacity as the Director of the Agency for the limited purpose of investigating M.K.'s assets, and for applying for Social Security and other benefits to which M.K. was apparently entitled. Counsel for M.K. was asked to inquire about M.K.'s desire to appear at a continued Hearing, and about her willingness to undergo an independent medical examination. The Hearing was continued to June 1, 1994.

In due course the Court was informed that M.K. did not desire a medical examination, and would not be attending the June 1, 1994 continued Hearing. Following that second Hearing, the Court, on June 6, 1994, ordered M.K. to appear

-2-

for an independent medical examination on June 20, 1994.
However, that Order was vacated on June 17, 1994 because
M.K. was escorted to the doctor's office by the Lehigh
County Sheriff's deputies on the morning of June 9, 1994. A
third Hearing was held on June 10, 1994, at which M.K. did
not appear, but was again represented by her Court-appointed
Counsel. As noted above, the Court issued its final Order
on June 13, 1994, making permanent the appointment of Mr.
Johnstone as the Limited Guardian of her person and estate.

The Court then, on June 14, 1994, appointed
attorney Gwin M. Krouse as the Guardian Ad Litem for M.K.,
for the sole purpose of advising the Court as to whether or
not the Court's Final Order of June 13, 1994 might be
stayed, pending an appeal to the Superior Court which it was
evident would be forthcoming. The Guardian met with her
Ward, and reported on June 17, 1994 that such a stay would
be appropriate. On July 1, 1994 the Court directed that the
Agency should refrain from carrying out any of its duties
until the thirty-day appeal period had run, unless that
became necessary to protect M.K. from imminent and
irreparable harm.

The appeal was filed on July 13, 1994, and the

-3-

Notes of Testimony were ordered transcribed. On August 15, 1994, the doctor was directed to provide a written report to the Court. The Notes of Testimony were completed on September 22, 1994.

## Findings of Fact

Dr. Joseph L. Antonowicz, M.D. a Board Certified Psychiatrist on the staff of a leading hospital, testified that he had examined M.K. at the request of the Agency, and had come to the conclusion that she suffered from a paranoid personality disorder. He described M.K. as having an excessive need to be self sufficient, to the point of making unreasonable choices. Her character includes an irrational fear of losing her independence, and an unreasonable mistrust of others. The doctor further gave his opinion that M.K.'s condition was fixed, with little likelihood that she would be able to trust her own therapist, should one be appointed for her. Doctor Antonowicz further testified that although M.K. is capable of communicating her needs to others, she does not do so as a result of her mistrustful paranoia. Thus, she is likely to harm herself through her own neglect. The Court finds the testimony of Dr.

-4-

Antonowicz entirely credible, particularly when coupled with the evidence offered by succeeding witnesses.

Agency personnel also testified at the Hearings, and related their involvement with M.K. over the past twenty years. Initially, M.K. was finding her way into the hallways of public buildings, where she would sleep, defecate and urinate. The Agency has taken several steps to aid M.K., including the securement of a place at the Lehigh County Home (known as Cedarbrook) from which she walked away, and the finding of a room at the Hotel Traylor (where she washed herself in the first-floor lobby bathroom instead of the bathroom which formed a part of her living unit). After those attempts failed, M.K. now attempts to groom herself by getting into gas station or restaurant bathrooms.

At present, M.K. is only able to walk very "hunched over". She smells of urine, and has severe venous ulcerations on her legs, from the knees down. She can barely walk, and has been banned from using the taxi cabs due to her urination in them in the past. She has also been banned from the County's Senior Citizens Center. She is 75 years old, and has lived "on the streets" for approximately the last 35 years of that lifetime. She panhandles for the

-5-

small amount of money she needs for her food, and accepts clothing donations. She is eligible for Social Security in the amount of $489.00 per month, but refuses to apply for those benefits. She has $3,918.00 in a local bank account. She wants to be "left alone".

At the Court's direction, against the wishes of M.K., Dr. Jane M. Borish performed a complete physical and an expansive mental status examination on June 9, 1994. Dr. Borish also treated M.K. with antibiotics, and reported that M.K. could not even walk alone. Rather than detail the Doctor's findings, the Trial Court would respectfully suggest that the Appellate Court refer to the transcript of the June 10, 1994 Hearing. The Doctor's findings were unrefuted, and are accepted as true. M.K. is no longer able to care for herself. She is beset with diseases, rashes and infections.

Although M.K. has children, the Court finds that they are unable to be a resource to M.K. The past efforts of her family to provide care have been rejected, and there is no evidence to suggest that she will take any direction from them. If the Court does not intervene, M.K. will undoubtedly fall victim to the weather, to disease, to a

-6-

broken hip, or will end up in prison due to her continued defiant trespasses. Her body is no longer resilient. She can no longer survive on the streets, and does not have the mentality to trust this community's responsible agencies to provide her needs for medical care and a safe place to sleep.

## Conclusions of Law

The Court is clearly convinced that M.K., due to her paranoia and distrustfulness, and due to her present extremely poor physical condition, is incapacitated, in that her ability to receive and evaluate information and to communicate decisions is significantly impaired.

M.K. is in need of a Limited Guardian of her Person and Estate as is set forth in the Court's Decree of June 13, 1994, which is attached hereto and which by this reference is incorporated as a part of this Opinion.

BY THE COURT:

Robert K. Young, Judge

Dated: September 29, 1994.

-7-

# Trial Judge: A Job Description

The Superior Court added a thoughtful and broader view to the M.K. decsision which follows.

> We are, of course, mindful that freedom from unwarranted governmental intrusion is a basic right which is protected by the Fourteenth Amendment. See, e.g., Santosky v. Kramer, 455 U.S. 745, 102 S.Ct. 1388, 71 L.Ed.2d 599 (1982). Thus, in cases such as this one, the courts must walk a fine line between depriving a citizen of her freedom and protecting that citizen from her own inability to care for herself. Nevertheless, we cannot, as a society, simply look the other way when one of our citizens is homeless and ill and unable to care for her physical needs because of a paranoid personality disorder. Although the present solution of appointing a guardian may not be the best solution in appellant's eyes, the alternative solution of doing nothing and allowing her to die in the street is certainly far worse.
>
> We note that the trial court has limited the guardian's powers and we fully approve of those limitations. Therefore, we affirm the trial court's order.
>
> Order affirmed.

# THE STATE HOSPITAL SITUATION

The Commonwealth, until more recent times, had taken direct care of thousands of men and women with debilitating mental illnesses. These individuals were provided shelter, food, clothing and medical care, all in a series of large State Hospitals. Such a hospital was located in Lehigh County at a place known as Rittersville, just east of the city of Allentown. As I am writing this job description the expansive tree lined campus sits empty of any patients. They exist, but they have been moved from a locked up institutional environment into smaller home-like facilities.

I mention the State Hospital, because one of my responsibilities was to review each patient's case, for the purpose of determining his or her continued need for the kind of restrictive living arrangements the State was then able to provide. A thoughtful Deputy Attorney General (Tom) made the necessary arrangements so that the Guardian ad Litem could interview each patient before I held a hearing at the State Hospital, again, without a robe. We spent several days a year at that job. We were trying to be sure that no abuse was occurring, and that the treatment being administered was the least intrusive and yet the most effective. Many of the patients were able to express themselves; some were not. The nursing staff also participated. They were helpful in describing daily care-taking problems, if any.

The yearly reviews led to only a few changes, but they did have at least two good effects. The fact that the Administrators and the staff of the hospital knew that their work was to some extent being evaluated, I hope and believe, gave them a feeling of useful importance. And, I know from listening to some of the patients, that they felt better being able to talk to their Guardian and me about their own individual situations and goals. As the doctors would say, those efforts probably did no harm. I thought those hearings were good for the patients, for the community to know about, and for me.

The Appointments of Guardians for Incapacitated Persons, mostly to aid the elderly, has increased significantly. The foregoing M. K. case was one of a relatively few such matters when I was handling those in the Orphans' Court in the period between 1984 and 1996. Then, there were more minors to protect than adults. The Administrative Office of Pennsylvania Courts reports that over the past ten years, Lehigh County's normal flow of Guardianships now produces 100-125 cases per year. The obvious factors that drive that change have been better health care leading to longer life, and, I suggest, that the families of the elderly are scattered, and that entitlement benefits need a responsible person or agency to process and to account for the expenditures.

# THE KALMBACH ESTATE: A NEW PARK

**M**ost of the cases I decided put the dispute to rest. Once I issued an Order somebody won and somebody lost. People moved on. That is how the court system is supposed to work. There were a few items, however, where what I ruled made a long-lasting difference to more than just the litigants. One of those involved the Kalmbach Estate I'll try to shorten a long story.

Mr. Frederick Kalmbach, an industrialist, owned a 22-acre farm/estate mostly in the little Borough of Macungie. At his death, he bequeathed a life estate of that property and other substantial assets to his son, with the proviso that at his son's death, the trustees of the remainder interest would, if feasible, turn the homestead, funded with the other assets, into a public park. After the son's death, the Trustees began to distribute the principal of the estate's funds to various charities. In their formal Accounting to the Court, they opined that there was not enough money to sustain a park.

The Accounting also revealed that one of the Trustees, William Simon, former United States Secretary of the Treasury, had indulged in some heavy self-dealing. He had, for example, pledged the sum of $150,000 to the University of Rochester, payable in three equal installments, to be used in that institution's William Simon school of Business. Some other large donations were made to Lehigh University and an institution of unknown pedigree in Botswana. No study about the feasibility of creating a park had been done.

I only had two choices of action. I could dismiss and surcharge the Trustees, or convince them to resign and appoint new fiduciaries. The solicitor for the Borough, then Thomas A. Wallitsch (now retired Judge Wallitsch) strongly advocated dismissal and redistribution. I asked him to wait a little which he did. Attorney William B. Butz had drawn the Will. He was one of the three Trustees. He was living in England in a rented castle. He expressed no objection to being replaced. A Mr. Dixon had been a tenant of the Kalmbach property, and was chosen as a Trustee so that he could attend to the upkeep of the property before it was sold. He had moved to Chicago. I do not think that he realized his delicate position. I made contact with him and told him that he too would be replaced. That left Secretary Simon who was then living in California. Following a conference with his New York attorneys, I was advised that he agreed to step down.

I knew that I had the power to remove all of them without asking. However, in this instance, my hope was that with some judicial restraint we could solve the problem without having the delays, expense and rancor that I saw coming if Simon decided to mount a defense. I was also thinking about the adverse effect upon Lehigh University, the University of Rochester and the other recipients who were faultless and counting on the pledged funds for ongoing programs. I did not disturb those grants already made or announced.

I appointed two new Trustees, John (Jack) G. Berrier, President of what was then known as the Lehigh County Community College, and Robert C. Dorney, President of Day Timers. They offered to serve without compensation for five-year staggered terms. The Bank remained to assume the investment duties. A Feasibility Study was undertaken that indicated that the establishment of a park was possible, if carried forward in modest steps. That is what was done. Today, the Kalmbach Memorial Park is an outstanding public facility that some of my Great-

Grandchildren are already enjoying due to the dedicated Park Administrators: first, Linda McCready, followed by Michael and Laura McCready.

# DR. SCHEIE: "OVER REACHING"

A second case of what I called "self-dealing" came before me in Orphans' Court, raising issues somewhat similar to the Kalmbach Estate. It involved an Accounting of the Trustees of the Paul Mackall and Evania Evans Bell Mackall Trust, which was created by the terms of the Last Will and Testament of Nina C. Mackall, Deceased. Nina died on March 4, 1981, leaving a substantial Estate, most of which she dedicated to a Trust with the specified purpose as follows:

> The Trust shall continue in perpetuity and shall exist and be operated to encourage and assist research into the causes, prevention, alleviation and cure of blindness and shall be dedicated entirely to charitable, educational and scientific purposes.

The will prohibited any of the income from being used "for the construction of buildings…administration expenses or scholarships other than those directly related to research in ophthalmology."

The Accounting covered the period during which the Trust had operated, namely from September 23, 1981 through December 31, 1990. The market value of the Trust was $8,528,363.16. During the 99 months of operation, the Trustees had made distributions and were seeking approval of the Court for their expenditures.

Nina, who died at the age of 88, had been a long-time patient and friend of Dr. Harold G. Scheie, an eminent ophthalmologist. Dr. Scheie was named as Trustee and given extraordinary power over the disposition of the Trust's income. During the six years of his service to the Trust, Dr. Scheie took $146,465.14 in commissions, and assumed the obligation to use the Trust's income "to encourage and assist research into the causes, prevention, and alleviation and cure of blindness."

Dr. Scheie was without a doubt a preeminent scholar in his field. Having approximately $3,000,000 of Mackall Trust income at his disposal, he authorized the expenditure of $468,309.00 directly to eye research projects. The other 86% of the income was either not distributed ($585,886.34); was used to provide capital to the University of Pennsylvania medical School or to his alma mater, the University of Minnesota Medical School, to establish or augment professional "chairs" ($1,190,000); and was used to create endowed Research Funds bearing the name of Nina Mackall at both of the above-named medical Schools ($453,009.81).

The remaining income was either not put to any use, or was paid over to the University of Pennsylvania or University of Minnesota Foundation, not for research, but as capital to create other research funds or endowed "chairs" for "research professionals." Dominating those grants, were an endowment of $500,000 to add to the Harold G. Scheie Research Professorship in Ophthalmology, and another grant to establish at the University of Minnesota, the Harold G.

Scheie Research Chair in Ophthalmology. Half of a million dollars was spent to create a "chair" for Elias Potter Lyon, and $140,000 to add to an existing "chair" in honor of Frank E. Burch. Drs. Lyon and Burch were mentors of Dr. Scheie in his earlier days at the University of Minnesota. The Lyon "chair" had never been filled at the time of my audit, then having unused income of $143,593.

Having detailed more financial information than you probably wanted to know (although there is a lot more), the conclusion at which I arrived, was that Dr. Scheie as Trustee, had crossed over the line of "tackiness" into the forbidden realm of self-dealing. He used the Mackall money to aggrandize himself. In his own Curriculum Vitae, he claims many lifetime accomplishments, and lists:

- The Harold G. Scheie Research Professorship established at The University of Pennsylvania – November 18, 1982
- Harold G. Scheie Chair in Ophthalmology, University of Minnesota, School of Medicine, Department of Ophthalmology – March 1987

No mention of Nina, Paul or Evania Mackall.

So, what did we do? And that "we" includes, once again, the Office of the Attorney General—represented by Senior Deputy Larry Barth—and my Administrative Counsel, Jan Thwaites. First, the Lawyers for the Estate of Dr. Scheie and for the corporate Trustee were indignant. They filed 54 exceptions to my Adjudication. (I believe that was a record.) Those were put on my next available Argument list, which gave us a few weeks to propose a proper remedy.

I had determined that Dr. Scheie's Trustee commissions were too high. The Superior Court rarely interferes with the Trial Court's findings in that area. Neither of the affected Universities had done anything wrong: Dr. Scheie had orchestrated the placement of the income. From the two days of testimony, it became evident that the Scheie name in the field of ophthalmology was a drawing card in recruiting bright new research associates. But I believed that the Mackall family's generosity ought to be acknowledged, and I also wanted, as stated in my Adjudication, "…to point out to the thousands of other trustees the high degree of selfless conduct, scrupulous good faith, and candor which is expected of all fiduciaries." I suppose I was guilty of "sending a message," but I was not imposing a different standard for Dr. Scheie, just reminding all fiduciaries of what was expected of them from the Orphans' Court. I was also thinking that the Scheie family would probably want no more adverse publicity regarding their luminary and might well entertain a reasonable compromise.

In due course, following a few conferences, the Scheie Estate agreed to the return of $71,344.43 of trustee fees; both Universities agreed to add the name of Nina Mackall to the "Chairs" and the Professorships; the Office of the Attorney General agreed, and I agreed.

# COURT ASSIGNMENTS: CRIMINAL COURT

Before discussing my work in Criminal Court my Great-Grandchildren might want to know why and how our judges divided the work. There were five judges in Lehigh County when I first began in mid-July of 1984. President Judge John E. Backenstoe and Judges Maxwell E. Davison, David E. Mellenberg, James N. Diefenderfer, and James Knoll Gardner. A sixth seat was vacant due to the early retirement of Martin J. Coyne. I filled that empty position and thus there were six. The consensus was that we did not prefer to specialize in any particular area, although there was some perceived efficiency with that method. Instead, we all agreed to take turns at serving in different Divisions. No one wanted to be stuck for too long in Family Court or the Criminal Division. I was asked to run the Orphans' Court because of my experience in that field, and because Judge Coyne had been doing only and all of that work, so that no one else had experience there. I was given one week a month to administer the Orphans' Court, but assignable to all of the other divisions. Now back to Criminal Court.

Luckily for my Great-Grandchildren, and for me, I have no copies of any of my Orders or Opinions arising out of criminal trials. In Criminal Court, there is a heavy volume and the cases normally move so quickly that all of the records are kept and managed by a fairly large staff of secretarial clerks. Stacks and more stacks of files were piled on a long, deep shelf beneath my bench, and as the cases were called I would be handed the proper file. If it was a Guilty Plea, I performed a standard conversation (called a Colloquy) with the defendant, going into his or her rights.

It did not take me long to figure out that I could move a lot more cases in Criminal Court if that "conversation" could be shortened. I prepared a rather long and complete list of a defendant's Constitutional protections (e.g. right to a lawyer, not to testify, burden of proof, cross examine witnesses, jury or bench trial, etc.). All of the items were then typed on a several-page form that I required be read and initialed by each defendant before I took his or her plea. I still had to ask the defendant a few questions to be sure that he was intelligent enough to understand what was on the form, but I believe that I saved at least five to six minutes on each case. I then verified from the defendant that the facts just given to me by the District Attorney were true.

In the years 2006-2015, the average number of new criminal cases filed in Lehigh County in each year was very close to 5,000. According to the Administrative Office of Pennsylvania Courts (AOPC), in 2015, 92% of the defendants either plead guilty or were allowed to enter special diversion disposition programs.

In some simple cases where the District Attorney and the defendant had come to a "Plea Bargain," I dictated the sentence right away to one of the very talented clerks, particularly Tina Beltz, and the case and its file went away.

In more serious cases, I ordered a "pre-sentence report." Those were prepared by the Probation Office. They contained details about the defendant's past criminal record, employment history, educational achievements, and sometimes facts about the crime at hand that had not come out at the plea bargain sidebar.

# SENTENCING IS ALMOST AN ART

Sentencing is almost an art. There are so many factors to consider. Not only what happened, but what was the effect on the victim? The victim's family? What are the ages of all of those involved? Is there a past history of criminal activity? Were weapons involved? Where did the crime occur? Were drugs or alcohol a factor? Does the defendant have any family support? What is the mental capacity and educational achievement of the defendant? Are there any minimum or maximum terms that relate to this crime? etc., etc. Once a fair term of incarceration comes to mind, if any, a judge needs to consider a term of and conditions of probation. Experience tells us that while most prisoners do well while staying in prison for the term imposed, a great many fail while on probation after jail. Probation is where the judicial system can do the most to rehabilitate.

Lehigh County has a dedicated Probation Department. The probation officers did their work in the field. They do not just sit at their desks waiting for a parolee to drop in for a visit. They visit the home and place of work of the probationer. If a condition of probation was to obtain a drug evaluation, followed by conforming to its recommendations, the probation officer would monitor the probationer's progress. A failure to keep up with a drug or alcohol plan was a violation of probation, which brought the offender back into court. He or she then faced possible additional incarceration.

The sentencing judge had a few tools to help during the probationary phase of a sentence. I could require an ankle bracelet, particularly when I had ordered her or him to stay away from some other person, or when they were given work release during specified hours. Portable alcohol breathalyzers were available that would not let a car start if the driver blew into it with alcohol in their breath. Depending upon the nature of the crime and the length of the jail time, Work Release was my favorite condition of probation, but the Department had to look hard for an employer with an appropriate job who was willing to hire a person on probation. At sentencing the term of probation varied. Again, it depended upon several factors. A long probationary period was used in cases where the defendant was ordered to make restitution for a substantial sum. That condition might reasonably take three or four years, and it was not fair to impose a condition that could not be achieved.

In some instances, I was not able to impose a condition that I thought might be appropriate. For example, some of the City cemeteries were in poor condition. My general thought is that a society that shows no respect for its ancestors is morally sick, but I was told that I could not use any probationers to work in the cemeteries, as that would be contrary to the Allentown municipal employees' union contract.

Not every condition of probation was an extension of punishment. In some cases, where the offender had been gainfully employed or was obviously employable, a condition of probation was that employment be found. In one case of mine, a long-time prostitute appeared before me for sentencing. As usual, I went through the pre-sentence dialogue with her, and as she answered my questions, I noticed that she had really bad teeth. She tried to hide them by talking through her hands. Otherwise, she appeared presentable. I had the thought that if the appearance of her teeth could be improved, she might be able to obtain more suitable employment. So, after asking whether the Probation Department could find sufficient money within its budget to restore them, I ordered as a condition of probation that her teeth be improved and that she find a regular job.

A poem of mine about the considerations involved in sentencing is included in the internet website noted in the appendix.

I do recall another criminal matter that caused some consternation. The arrest for a traffic violation by the police of one of the Whitehall Townships (there are three) was challenged. A conviction would entail the loss of the driver's license to operate a motor vehicle. The defense counsel had heard a rumor that the police department was quietly attempting to bolster its budget by issuing a substantially increased number of tickets. He called the Chief of Police to the stand. Following strong cross-examination, the Chief admitted that his department was given a "Quota" of violations to fill. That is illegal in Pennsylvania, and I therefore dismissed the charges. Other members of the defense bar learned of my order and were thereafter able to void a number of traffic arrests.

Search and Seizure cases required a special attitude for me. I had to focus on the law as laid out by the appellate courts. Never mind the fact that a gun or drugs had actually been found in possession of the defendant. The issue was how the police obtained those items. Now I understood the Fourth Amendment, but it was quite unpleasant to have to rule that the incriminating evidence could not be used in court, the result of which was normally a guilty person going free. I just had to swallow that pill and remind myself that "the right of the people to be secure in their persons, houses, papers, and effects, against unreasonable searches and seizures" was worth protecting in full. No one wanted a police state: we all desired our privacy.

The pre-sentence reports also included the minimum and maximum sentences that were permitted under legislation. Those restrictions always bothered me. It seemed to me that sentencing lengths ought to be a judicial function. We pride ourselves on sentencing individuals, not classes of people. But I was stuck with the system given to me. My small protest was not to look at the recommended sentence until I had come to my own conclusion. I must admit, however, that the Probation officers were on the money or very close to my separate ideas as to the appropriate duration of a prison or probation sentence (with time served, if any).

# THE HARVEY ROBINSON APPEAL

In my file of seventy-one appealed cases, I only found one criminal matter. That appeal was a mandatory one. The Supreme Court of Pennsylvania must review every sentence of death. I inherited the trial of a Mr. Harvey Robinson from Judge Diefenderfer, who became ill just before a jury was to be assembled. He had heard and decided all the pretrial motions. Robinson was alleged to have raped a woman, and murdered in serial fashion four young girls. The facts were gruesome. The case was well publicized, which made the jury selection process long and difficult. We eventually obtained 14 suitable jurors (two were alternates). District Attorney Robert L. Steinberg (now Judge Steinberg) presented the Commonwealth's case in a fair and determined manner to the point that the jury found Robinson guilty of the rape and all four first-degree murders. My Great-Grandchildren do not need to know more, except that the trial of Robinson was also a trial for me—full courtroom; a dozen witnesses including the rape victim; expert witnesses; extra sheriffs to protect Robinson from members of the families of the victims and to keep him subdued; and many evidentiary rulings.

The jury found that the mitigating circumstances did not outweigh the aggravating circumstances, and recommended death sentences for the murders. Under law, we do not put the duty of sentencing on the jury, but put that responsibility on the trial judge. Having heard all of the testimony, I without reservation sentenced Robinson to the maximum State prison term for the rape, and then I sentenced him to death on each of the four separate murders, consecutively. That might be considered overkill, but what it meant was that if there was an error to one of the charges at any stage of the pretrial or trial, that error would not affect the other death sentences.

And that is what happened. The United States Supreme Court, well after the Robinson trial, ruled that if a defendant committed a crime before his or her 18th birthday, a death sentence below that age constituted a cruel and unusual punishment. The Court made that decision retroactive. Robinson was two weeks short of his 18th birthday when he committed the first murder. His sentence on that offense was later reduced to life in prison. He is still sitting in death row – for over twenty years.

A little side story about the Robinson case:

The District Attorney, Defense Counsel and I, all agreed that we did not want the jury to see Robinson in the arm and leg chains that the sheriff used to bring him from the prison into the courtroom. We wanted him seated with just his ankle chains on which would be hidden under the defense table. His hand and arms would be free when the jury saw him. The solution was to get the jury into the jury deliberating room, and then bring him through my office, where there was a back door into the courtroom. At recesses or at the end of the day, Harvey would need to wait until the jury left the courtroom. The first day of trial, my then law clerk, Anne Friday, was sitting at her desk in my office. She heard shuffling and the clanking of Robinson's chains, and to her surprise saw him with two deputy sheriffs coming down the hallway. They passed very close to her. She has not forgotten the staring glare that Robinson gave to her. She claims that he reappeared a few times in nightmares. I had forgotten to tell her about the plan.

# THE PLACEMENT OF LAW CLERKS

The placement of my law clerk's desk in my office ("chambers" sounds too pretentious) worked out well for both of us. Whatever I wanted to discuss, she or he was there. The law clerks were and are fully qualified attorneys. In my view, law clerks are lawyers for the judge. They are fresh out of law school, where they excelled, and are up to date with the latest changes to the law. My clerks told me that they appreciated being where they could see and hear what was happening.

When I was on the bench, they did the necessary telephone scheduling and worked on editing my Opinions.

# THE SNOW TRACKS CASE

Getting back to my work in the Criminal Court, I can remember two cases that were relatively unimportant, but interesting to me, and may be to you.

Following a moderate snowstorm, a local convenience store was robbed. No one saw the perpetrator. The police were called and upon their arrival noticed snow tracks of shoes leading away from the premises. They were able to follow the shoe tracks for several blocks when the indentations came to the door of an apartment building. Police entered the common hallway and followed wet marks on the floor that led to a particular door. They knocked on that door and were permitted entrance by someone who gave permission to look around, which the police did. In a bedroom closet was a pair of wet boots. The person who was identified as the one using that room was arrested and charged. He pled not guilty. A jury was impaneled and the case went to trial. The police were praised for their quick response; the Defendant was found guilty and punished, and I finally had a wonderful depiction to use in describing "circumstantial evidence" to future juries.

# A CASE OF JURY NULLIFICATION

The second case (with Attorney Henry S. Perkin, now a Federal Magistrate, prosecuting) still bothers me a little bit. It involved the criminal charge of "Theft of Services." The Defendant went to an electronic supply store and purchased a legal television decoding box. By plugging it into an electrical outlet and then attaching it to a television set, the user was able to watch certain cable channels that otherwise required a fee. The cable company instigated the proceedings, which the District Attorney's office agreed to prosecute. The Defendant pled not guilty.

A jury was selected. It contained a proper mix of young and old, male and female, with a variety of occupations. Mr. Perkin presented his case flawlessly. He produced authenticated receipts for the purchase of the unit, as well as a qualified expert to explain its function. He established the loss of income to the cable company. He argued that if this conduct persisted it would increase the costs to other lawful cable subscribers. The Defendant did not testify. Defense Counsel did not challenge anything, except to argue that his client should not be punished for a situation where it is permissible for a store to sell something that no one is allowed to use, and, that "everybody was doing it."

In a civil case, I could have granted a Motion for Summary Judgment. That is, the facts were undisputed, and under the law the plaintiff would be entitled to receive damages. But in criminal law the defendant is entitled to receive the verdict of a jury. That jury had to decide if there was a theft. Of course, there was a theft and my jury charge left no doubt about that. The jury came back with a "Not Guilty" verdict.

Now what bothers me, is that such a "jury nullification" action comes with real danger to our fundamental democratic system of the "rule of law." As a judge, I had to follow the law on several occurrences when I believed the law to be wrong. The jury took an oath to obey the law, but did not. I understand that a jury nullification verdict is, in essence, the people speaking against the established authority, but it should not be encouraged. There are better ways to protest.

I noted that nullification bothered me a little bit, because it is so rare. There is an interesting precedent that I will repeat for my Great-Grandchildren.

In 1670, the founder of our Commonwealth, William Penn, was arrested for Participating in an Unlawful Assembly. It is also reported that he refused to don his hat when required. He was one of those troublesome Quakers. Following unrefuted testimony, the Judge directed the jury to retire and to find Mr. Penn guilty. The jury declared him not guilty anyway. The Judge then put the jury in prison! Justice was quickly restored when the lower court was reversed by the Common Pleas Court. For some unknown reason the case is designated as "Bushel's Case."

# THE O'NEAL VS. OSBORNE CASE: AN AUTOMOBILE COLLISION

For the sake of variety and hoping to hold your interest in knowing what goes on in a trial judge's workday, I am turning back to the Civil Division, with two of the cases I decided involving cars. I wonder if my Great-Grandchildren will still drive automobiles, or whether by then robotic vehicles will swarm driver-free. This shifting between various legal subjects in a haphazard way is my attempt to replicate the actual somewhat disjointed schedule of work of trial judges—or at least of this trial judge.

Car collision cases did not involve very much of my time. A large percentage of those, probably 70%, consisted of unresolved disputes between two or more automobile insurance companies. Pennsylvania has long required car owners to have liability insurance. There are issues about which carrier owes excess coverage, or non-insured coverage, or underinsured coverage.

There remains the absurdity of requiring a mistrial if it is even hinted to the jury that one or more of the parties are covered with insurance, when everyone knows that they all have it. Most often the insurance has been paid, and the company who paid it goes to court in an effort to get another company to contribute. Sometimes, there are uncompensated damages for pain and suffering which do need to be settled. I will discuss the impact of a jury learning about insurance coverage later.

The following short cases do not require any explanation, but I think you might appreciate the interesting factual situations they depict. We do not yet know whether the law or juries will hold the manufacturers of driverless cars, the passive non-drivers or the suppliers of the computers and sensors responsible.

IN THE COURT OF COMMON PLEAS OF LEHIGH COUNTY, PENNSYLVANIA

CIVIL ACTION - LAW

| | | |
|---|---|---|
| TRACY O'NEAL, | ) | |
| Plaintiff | ) | |
| | ) | |
| vs. | ) | No. 90-C-1447 |
| | ) | |
| THOMAS OSBORNE, | ) | |
| Defendant | ) | |

## ORDER

NOW, this 19 day of _November_, 1993, upon consideration of the written Briefs and oral Argument of Counsel, and consistent with the accompanying footnote,

IT IS ORDERED that Defendant's Motion for a New Trial is Denied.[1]

BY THE COURT:

Robert K. Young, Judge

---

[1]This case arose out of an automobile accident in Dover, Delaware on July 5, 1988. The Defendant, Thomas Osborne (Defendant), was driving a vehicle directly behind an automobile in which Plaintiff, Tracy O'Neal (Plaintiff), was a passenger. While in a line of traffic stopped for a red light on Route 113 North, the Defendant's vehicle was

CONTINUATION OF FOOTNOTE

---

"nudged" from behind. After briefly looking in his rearview mirror, the Defendant looked forward and was unable to stop his automobile before striking the rear end of the Plaintiff's vehicle. Due to this impact, the Plaintiff allegedly sustained injuries to her neck, which became apparent several days later. On July 3, 1990, the Plaintiff filed a negligence action against the Defendant for personal injuries stemming from this accident.

A jury trial was held on December 10 and 11, 1992. The jury specifically found that the Defendant was not negligent, and the Plaintiff has filed Post-Trial Motions briefing two issues.

The Plaintiff's first argument is that the jury's verdict was against the clear weight of the evidence, requiring a new trial. The decision whether to grant a new trial based on a challenge as to the weight of the evidence is within the sound discretion of the trial court. Thompson v. City of Philadelphia, 507 Pa. 592, 493 A.2d 669 (1985); Commonwealth v. Murray, 408 Pa. Super. 435, 597 A.2d 111 (1991). It is well established that a new trial should be awarded on the basis that the verdict is against the weight of the evidence when the jury's verdict is so contrary to the evidence as to shock one's sense of justice, and to make the award of a new trial imperative, so that right may be given another opportunity to prevail. Commonwealth v. Whitney, 511 Pa. 232, 512 A.2d 1152 (1986); Insurance Co. of the State of Pennsylvania v. Miller, ___ Pa. Super. ___, 627 A.2d 797 (1993).

The jury heard testimony presented by both parties concerning the accident, in addition to being read two relevant sections of the Delaware Motor Vehicle Code regarding the correct speed and appropriate space which must be maintained between vehicles. After hearing all of this evidence, the jury obviously chose to believe the Defendant's explanation of the events; namely, that the reason his vehicle struck the Plaintiff's automobile in the rear was because his own vehicle was "nudged" from the back by the car directly behind him. The verdict of "not

-2-

CONTINUATION OF FOOTNOTE

---

negligent" is not so contrary to the evidence as to shock one's sense of justice, as was the case of Haines v. Neshamony Mechanical, Inc., 9 D. & C. 4th 538 (1991), upon which the Plaintiff relies. In Haines, the jury ignored unequivocal evidence of Defendant's negligence that Defendant's employee conceded that on a snowy roadway he lost control of his vehicle and crossed over onto the Plaintiff's side of the roadway. He testified that (1) his automobile was in perfect condition; (2) he saw the snow and ice; (3) he slowed down; but (4) he slid into the oncoming lane of travel. He offered no excuse.

In the case before us, the Defendant presented evidence that his attention was momentarily diverted due to his vehicle being struck in the rear, causing him to look in his rearview mirror, instead of forward. It is reasonable for the jury to have found that this "nudging" created an emergency, not by his own doing, and that a reasonably prudent driver would also look in the mirror to see what was wrong. That evidence, if believed, is sufficient to refute Plaintiff's allegations of negligence.

The second issue concerns the jury charge. The Plaintiff contends that the following jury instruction was improper:

> If you find no negligence, if you think
> that what he said was, that he was
> nudged, he looked up and a reasonable
> and prudent person would do that, then
> you find no fault. [N.T. 12/11/92 at 74]

In ruling upon a Court's charge, it is well established in Pennsylvania that the charge must be looked at in its entirety. Alleged errors in jury instructions cannot be taken out of context, but rather must be considered in relation to the entire charge, and in light of the evidence present. Albert v. Alleter, 252 Pa. Super. 203, 381 A.2d 459 (1977); Soda v. Baid, 411 Pa. Super. 80, 600 A.2d 1274 (1991); and Sedlitsky v. Pareso, ___ Pa. Super. ___, 625 A.2d 71 (1993).

-3-

CONTINUATION OF FOOTNOTE

---

Defendant testified that he was momentarily distracted when he was "nudged" from behind. However, when he looked forward, his vehicle struck the rear end of Plaintiff's automobile. Plaintiff urges that this evidence is not a legally sufficient basis for the Court to give the above-quoted charge. Plaintiff argues that even though the Defendant was "nudged" and looked up, he still had a duty to control his vehicle before colliding into the rear of Plaintiff's vehicle, making the charge erroneous.

This argument is in reality a motion for a directed verdict on the issue of liability, and ignores the often-stated concept that not every accident involves negligence. Accidents involving bee stings, sun glare, sudden patches of ice, torrential rain, and other unforeseen circumstances are some examples where the law permits a jury to find that the operator confronted with such perils are not negligent. They acted, it can be argued, reasonably under the conditions then existing. See innumerable cases in West's Pennsylvania Digest, 2d, Vol. 44, Sec. 12.

The Plaintiff's third reason in support of its Motion for a New Trial was not briefed, and will, therefore, not be considered.

-4-

# LEAR VS. HARTMAN

IN THE COURT OF COMMON PLEAS OF LEHIGH COUNTY, PENNSYLVANIA

CIVIL ACTION - LAW

DAVID G. LEAR,                    )
                                  )
          Plaintiff               )
                                  )
     v.                           )    No. 88-C-2328
                                  )
ANNETTE C. HARTMAN,               )
                                  )
          Defendant               )

\* \* \* \* \*

APPEARANCES:

    KEITH R. PAVLACK, ESQUIRE,
    And with him, CHARLES C. HANSFORD
    & ASSOCIATES, P.C.
       On behalf of the Plaintiff.

    KENT H. HERMAN, ESQUIRE,
    And with him, KING, McCARDLE, HERMAN & FREUND,
       On behalf of the Defendant.

\* \* \* \* \*

OPINION

ROBERT K. YOUNG, Judge.

On September 8, 1987, David G. Lear (David), was driving his automobile in a northbound direction on Route 309 near the Parkland High School in South Whitehall Township, Lehigh County. It was raining very heavily.

Although it was near the noon hour, David's headlights were on, as were his windshield wipers. He was travelling at a speed of approximately 30 miles per hour on a straight stretch of two-lane highway in his own lane of travel when he saw the automobile of the Defendant (Annette) cross the yellow line and collide with his vehicle. Annette also testified that her car crossed over the yellow center line and that the accident occurred in David's lane of traffic.

A jury trial resulted in a verdict in favor of Annette. The jury specifically found that she had not been negligent. Unrefuted evidence established that it was raining so violently that the Community College which Annette had been attending that morning cancelled its afternoon classes. Annette explained that as she was travelling south on the straight and level road, her car simply skidded over to the left and into David's vehicle. She was in a line of traffic, not following closely behind the car ahead of her. She did not apply the brakes too hard. The police investigation resulted in no charges of violating any motor vehicle regulations, it being the opinion of the officer that it was the torrential rainfall and consequential poor visibility that had caused the

-2-

accident.

David argues that the Trial Court should have charged the jury that Annette was negligent as a matter of law. Based upon Bohner v. Stine, 316 Pa.Super. 426, 463 A.2d 438 (1983), the Court utilized Standard Instruction 3.31, and explained that it was the jury's function to determine whether Annette had violated any motor vehicle code sections. Unlike Bohner, where the Defendant had admitted that he had hit the brakes too hard, in this case there were no specific acts of mismanagement of the vehicle in evidence. Bohner indicates that the Trial Court is not to instruct the jury to find negligence unless the facts are so clear that no two minds could differ. In this case, the police attributed the cause of the accident to the extraordinary weather, and this Trial Judge has neither the courage nor inclination to attribute a lack of reason to investigating officers.

The jury was instructed that the burden of proof had shifted to Annette to explain her presence on the wrong side of the roadway. They were satisfied with the truth of her version of what happened, and found no negligence. It is axiomatic that not every mishap or accident involves

-3-

negligent conduct. Unanticipated ice, bright sunlight, and flooding do occur on the highways, and it is only when the operator of a vehicle acts unreasonably in facing these extraordinary circumstances that fault can be attributed to the driver.

BY THE COURT:

Robert K. Young, Judge

Dated: *January 4, 1993*

# A WASTE OF THE COURT'S TIME

I am sure that by now you have come to understand that a trial judge's time is important. There were cases waiting in line. Thus, it was annoying when time was wasted. In the case of K. L. R. vs. S. M. R., wife K. refused to pay court costs in a Protection From Abuse case in the amount of $20.25 although gainfully employed after the couple reconciled. I ordered payment after a hearing. She took an appeal to the Superior Court. My decision was affirmed, but only after I was required to prepare an Opinion and after three Superior Court judges reviewed the record and wrote their own Memorandum. I will not waste your time in reading both decisions.

# THE CITY OF ALLENTOWN TAX LEVY CASE

A bigger waste of my time was made by the City of Allentown. I do sound a bit petulant in my Opinion, but those "in-the-know" told me that the City's plan was to be able to blame the Court for the tax increase.

IN THE COURT OF COMMON PLEAS OF LEHIGH COUNTY, PENNSYLVANIA
CIVIL ACTION - LAW

IN RE: CITY OF ALLENTOWN,           :
       PENNSYLVANIA                  :      NO. 86-C-2707
       TAX LEVY FOR 1987             :

ORDER

AND NOW, this 31st day of December, 1986, pursuant to Section 37531 of the Third Class City Code, 53 P.S. 37531 (57, upon proper notice by publication and posting; and following a Hearing held on this day, the Court finds that by competent and credible evidence the Petitioner (City of Allentown) has met its burden of proof by a preponderance of evidence that the additional millage of 1.2846 mills over and above twenty-five (25) mills is necessary to meet the monetary obligations imposed by its approved budget.[1]

Accordingly, it is ORDERED that the City of Allentown, Pennsylvania, is authorized to levy a rate of taxation in the total amount of 26.2846 mills for the fiscal/calendar year 1987.

By the Court:

_____ J.

1 On December 17, 1986, the Council of the City of Allentown, by a 5-1 vote, approved by Ordinance No. 12750, a 1987 City Budget which requires a millage levy in excess of the 25 mills

-1-

normally permitted by law. On the same date and by the same vote City Council approved Ordinance No. 12751 (Section 1.) which actually levied the tax millage of 2.62846 dollars on each One Hundred Dollars ($100.00) of assessed valuation of taxable property. Paragraph (5) of Section 37531 of the Third Class City Code, 53 P.S. 37531, states;

> Where the City Council by a majority action shall, upon due cause shown, petition the Court of Quarter Sessions for the right to levy additional millage, the Court, after such public notice as it may direct and after hearing, may order a greater rate than twenty-five mills but not exceeding five additional mills to be levied.

The Pennsylvania Commonwealth Court in City of

Altoona v. Central Pa. Retiree's Assn., 510 A. 2d. 868 (1986)

instructs the Hearing Court at page 870 as follows:

> While the statute gives the trial court the discretion to determine from the record whether due cause exists to warrant additional millage, it does not invite the court to examine the budget itself and re-view the wisdom of the legislative decision underlying its adoption. Such legislative decisions cannot be disturbed absent a clear abuse of discretion. See Davis v. City of Connellsville, 49 Pa. Common-wealth Ct. 106, 410 A.2d 937 (1980). As stated earlier, we believe that the trial court's factual determination under Section 2531(5) is limited solely to the issue of whether the additional millage is necessary given the requirements of the approved budget. The City meets its burden of proof when it can show by competent credible evidence that its anticipated revenues will be insufficient to meet the monetary obligations imposed by its approved budget.

It is apparently the Court's duty in this type of case to

provide an additional public forum at public expense; to

determine whether the mathematics of the City's budget are

-2-

correct; to assure that a full and complete disclosure has been made under oath of the categories of income and expense; and to ascertain that the basis on which the City determined its calculations are reasonable and not patently in error. The wisdom of the legislative policies underlying the budgetary decisions are beyond our power to review.

More than four hours of testimony, nine exhibits, and four witnesses were heard by the Court and public. The professionals in charge of the City's fiscal affairs testified fairly and frankly which the Court appreciated. Counsel for the City presented oral argument, and the Court is convinced that if the City is to meet the obligations set forth in the budget already approved by City Council, the imposition of the requested millage increase is <u>necessary</u>.

The word "necessary" is emphasized because there is great doubt that these proceedings were required. The City's budget administrator warned as early as February of 1986 that a severe budget deficit was impending in a five-column Section B front page article in this County's largest newspaper. Many similar press releases issued by the City, continued throughout the year, to the extent that the administrator gained the nickname "Prophet of Doom". The various exhibits introduced by the City clearly show that the present need for the millage increase has been perceived and made public for almost a year.

To avoid the last minute use of our busy Court

system the City simply needed to adopt a higher tax ratio. For many years Allentown established a predetermined ratio of 60% of the market valuation supplied by the County.  In 1974 by Ordinance No. 12092 the City elected a 50% ratio, and as a part of that ordinance stated "...provided however, that the City may at any time select a different predetermined ratio."  Testimony adduced at the hearing established that with a ratio of approximately 60% the City's millage would not need to be set above the 25 mill limit in 1987, and, that due in part to the County's new assessment reevaluation program the financial problems being encountered at the present millage level should be alleviated.  In the <u>City of Altoona</u> case the ratio was already at the maximum 100%.  In short, whether we approve of the increase in millage, or the City changes from a 50% ratio to a 60% ratio, will not make any meaningful difference to the "bottom line" due by the taxpayers.

Were it not for the fact that there is now apparently insufficient time for the City to change the ratio (which on past occasions was accomplished in March and August) the Court would deny the City's petition on the basis that the City has the means within its own power to cure the problem without the necessity of involving the Courts.  However, counsel has persuasively argued that such a denial might cause confusion to its taxpayers upon the arrival of their

-4-

bills, some increase in assessment appeals and possible
additional expense.  The Court's acquiescence in granting
the City's Petition is limited to this instance and is not
intended to set a precedent.

# WHERE DO CASES GO ON APPEAL?

Cases in which a municipality or the Commonwealth or one of its agencies are a litigant are appealable to the Commonwealth Court. All others are "sent up" if appealed to our State's Superior Court. Those Judgments are "handed down." The Supreme Court of Pennsylvania hears what it wants to hear (as does the Supreme Court of the United States). Those highest Courts, in selecting cases, tend to focus on matters of State or National importance and overseeing that there is consistency of case law among the lower courts.

# "TAKING JUDICIAL NOTICE": LOWER MACUNGIE TOWNSHIP RECLASSIFICATION

From time to time, we were obliged to decide cases involving local governments – Cities, Boroughs, and Townships. Most often these cases concerned challenges to their zoning boards, but again, variety prevailed. In the upcoming reclassification case, it might be helpful to know the key dates of the legal events. I was sitting in Motion Court on August 2, 1995. Counsel for a group of residents of Lower Macungie Township (Lehigh County) presented a Petition, asking the Court to direct the Lehigh County Board of Elections to place on the November 7, 1995 election ballot, a question as to whether or not the Township should become a Township of the First Class. Brief testimony was taken in Motion Court. I was satisfied that there were sufficient petitioners and signed the proposed Order. Another resident of the Township filed a Request to Reconsider. I did reconsider, but on October 2, 1995, issued my Opinion affirming my initial grant of the Reclassification Petition. The Resident-Objector filed an appeal to the Commonwealth Court on September 1, 1995. On October 2, 1995 that body found that the appeal was untimely and dismissed the case. There was still time to place the question on the November ballot. You will see that in some fairly isolated situations, a judge may "take judicial notice" of facts not of record.

IN THE COURT OF COMMON PLEAS OF LEHIGH COUNTY, PENNSYLVANIA

CIVIL ACTION - LAW

IN RE: )
)
THE MATTER OF THE ) No. 95-C-1778
RECLASSIFICATION OF )
LOWER MACUNGIE TOWNSHIP )

ORDER

NOW, this 25ᵗʰ day of August, 1995,

IT IS ORDERED that the Motion for Reconsideration is denied.[1]

BY THE COURT:

Robert K. Young, Judge

---

[1]The Motion/Petition of a resident of Lower Macungie Township to Reconsider this Court's Order of August 2, 1995 raises the issue of whether or not the failure of the Lehigh County Commissioners to certify the fact that Lower Macungie Township has a population of three hundred inhabitants to the square mile necessitates the setting aside of the Court's Order of August 2, 1995. That Order directed the Lehigh County Board of Elections to place upon the ballot a question regarding the wishes of the electorate to become a Township of the First Class. This Court takes judicial notice of the fact that the 1990 United States census indicates a population for Lower Macungie Township of 16,871. The Lehigh/Northampton Joint Planning Commission places the land area of that Township at 22.9. Thus, the population per square mile is 736. The failure of the County Commissioners to certify those facts, intentionally or unintentionally, can not be used to frustrate the right of the owners of more than 25% of the real value of the Township to ask the voters to consider becoming a Township of the First Class.

# A WORD OR TWO ABOUT "ARGUMENT COURT"

"Argument Court" is where most legal issues that came before me were decided. Almost every serious case contained the seeds of a debate about some legal question. These questions often arose upon a litigant filing a Motion. For example, following the filing of a Complaint the defendant might respond with a Motion for Summary Judgment, or for a more specific Complaint, or perhaps a demurrer on the basis of jurisdiction or standing. Any such motion needed to be answered by a judge. Typically, that happened by putting the case on the Argument list for a certain date, with briefs due beforehand. I estimate that about eight to ten individual arguments could be heard in a morning's work, with that many more in the afternoon.

The briefs were received by me several days before Argument. My law clerk and I would read them and make some preliminary notes, including any questions that seemed germane. The actual arguments were presented to me orally by each side in turn. The lawyers stood while presenting their positions and sat at counsel table when the other side was talking. The issues were usually of a serious nature, many times hinging upon questions that could involuntarily end the case. I quickly learned not to decide anything until the debate was over.

I took a lot of short notes in almost every Trial, Hearing or Conference, sufficient for me to produce a footnote to an Order. The appellate courts required an opinion. So, as you have probably discovered, I often just created an opinion by sending up a one-sentence statement that my footnote as attached was my Opinion. Sometimes I added to the footnote if, after receiving the reasons for the appeal, I thought I should address a point or two responding to those reasons I had not covered in the original footnote.

My Court Crier had the list of matters for the day, and would let the attorneys know about when their case was due to be heard, although quite a few stayed after the call of the list to listen to the earlier arguments. A day of Arguments was a day of learning—particularly for me. I always ended their presentations with a thank you, but I do not think that the lawyers really comprehended the fact that in my view, they were helping me.

Occasionally a lawyer became so intense about winning that he or she began to argue heatedly with the other lawyer. I would then immediately admonish them and remind them that they were in a courtroom where all questions and comments were to be addressed to the court. That usually worked to cool down the rhetoric. I can only recall two times when I had the Court Crier abruptly adjourn court for a fifteen-minute recess for a cooling-off period.

# A ZONING BOARD APPEAL:
# TOTH VS. ALLENTOWN ZONING BOARD

My law clerks saved six zoning cases, the most of any category from which I was appealed. The litigants in this area of law are rather territorial, as is probably the same everywhere. That is, we all feel a keen interest about the neighborhood in which we live. Any encroachment on the way things are is deemed a threat. And, neighbors often get together to raise enough money to hire an attorney.

Each community has a board of appointed citizens who hear and decide questions about the town's zoning ordinance. In those disputes, it is the practice that the trial court does not take testimony. We rely on the members of the zoning board and their solicitor to ask the right questions, receive all of the relevant exhibits, make findings of fact, and interpret their own zoning ordinance. The boards are "quasi-judicial." In those events where their decisions are appealed to us, we only overrule them if they make an error of law, abuse their discretion or find facts that are not substantiated in the record. The result of our present system is to keep local zoning problems pretty much in the hands of the local citizens. They are the ones who live with the zones and the rules established by their local elected officials (council members of cities and boroughs and township supervisors).

IN THE COURT OF COMMON PLEAS OF LEHIGH COUNTY, PENNSYLVANIA

CIVIL ACTION - LAW

LASZLO TOTH,                          )
                                      )
          Appellant                   )
                                      )
     vs.                              )
                                      )
CITY OF ALLENTOWN ZONING              )
HEARING BOARD,                        )     No. 83-C-3527
                                      )
          Appellee                    )
                                      )
     and                              )
                                      )
HARRY C. WEIL, III and                )
LORETTA L. WEIL,                      )
                                      )
          Intervenors                 )


                    *  *  *  *  *  *  *


APPEARANCES:

          ROBERT W. BROWN, ESQUIRE,
             with him, BROWN, BROWN & SOLT,
             On behalf of Intervenors.

          THOMAS F. TRAUD, JR., ESQUIRE,
             with him, ROBERTS, TRAUD, WALLITSCH & CORKERY,
             On behalf of Appellant.

FRANCIS P. BURIANEK, ESQUIRE,
    with him CITY SOLICITOR'S OFFICE,
    On behalf of Appellee.

* * * * * * *

O P I N I O N

ROBERT K. YOUNG, Judge.

This case concerns an appeal sought from the decision of the Zoning Hearing Board of the City of Allentown, Lehigh County, Pennsylvania, dated November 23, 1983. The Board on that date approved the Intervenor/Petitioner's application both to expand the facilities and to allow a non-conforming use of the premises.

Appellant, a neighbor of the property involved, claims that the Board's decision was arbitrary, capricious, an abuse of discretion and contrary to law.

The premises involved, known as 817-827 South Corn Street, Allentown, Pennsylvania, is currently used for the repair of automobiles. The owners of the property (hereinafter referred to as the Petitioner), who on February 21, 1984 took title under a long-term purchase agreement,

-2-

have so used the property since some time prior to 1973. In
January, 1973 the Allentown Zoning Hearing Board denied a
similar application of the Petitioner. However, the
Petitioner has been continuing to use the premises for this
non-conforming use without permission up to the present
time.

The Allentown Zoning Hearing Board held a public
hearing on November 21, 1983 upon Petitioner's application
for a zoning variance. At such hearing, the Board
investigated the use, the past uses, and the real estate
potential of the property. The Board found that (1) The
building was originally constructed for business use, and
had been used sporadically as an automobile repair shop, (2)
The Petitioner has made recent improvements to the property
in an attempt to improve upon the unsightliness of the lot,
(3) The contemplated expansion of the premises would further
improve the lot's appearance, (4) The contemplated fence
would deter neighborhood children from playing on the
premises, a danger of concern to the Objectors at the
hearing, and (5) The property could not be sold, except for

-3-

the use contemplated.

The Allentown Zoning Hearing Board further found that the property could not be used for strictly residential purposes; a hardship would result to the owner of the property if the application was denied; and that approval of such application would not adversely affect the public safety, welfare or interest. The Board approved the application, based upon twelve conditions imposed upon the Petitioner to assure that the lot's appearance would be improved and that the dangers resulting from the contemplated use would be alleviated. Such conditions concerned, inter alia, limited hours of operation, fencing, shrub lines and automobile entrances, as well as specific operations of the business.

Our inquiry in this appeal of the Board's decision is limited. We must only determine if the discretion vested in that Board has been abused. We are not permitted to substitute our decision for that of the Board's, but solely to rule on the issue of whether or not the Zoning Board abused the discretion given to it. If the Board's decision

-4-

was neither arbitrary, capricius, unreasonable, nor in violation of law, then we have no choice but to affirm its action. <u>Ruch v. Zoning Board</u> 28 Leh. Co. L.J. 5 (1957); <u>Border Appeal</u> 369 Pa. 517 (1952).

We have carefully reviewed the twelve (12) conditions imposed upon the grant of this variance, together with the Notes of Testimony, record papers and briefs. We are concerned with the misbehavior of the Petitioner in continuing to use the property in violation of the Zoning Ordinance for over ten (10) years. However, this is not an Equity case and the apparent lack of enforcement by the City is not before this Court. We also find that the Zoning Board is not bound by its prior 1973 disallowance of the request for similar relief by the same Petitioner relating to the same premises. Different circumstances may have prevailed in 1983; new conditions have been added; the testimony of witness both pro and con have changed, and in any event, a successor Board is free to reevaluate its prior decisions.

We find that the Allentown Zoning Hearing Board

did not abuse its discretion in granting Petitioner's application for a variance. The Board investigated the relevant circumstances concerning the use and structure of the involved premises, and its detailed Order is indicative of the thoroughness employed in this matter.

Having found no abuse of discretion, the appeal is denied.

The Toth case above is fairly typical of the zoning cases that came before us. There usually seemed to be some "sticking points" which encouraged disappointed objectors to file an appeal. In Toth, the "sticking points" were, of course, the flaunting of the non-conforming use for ten years and the prior ruling of an earlier board. However, Zoning Boards are given discretion, and I did not believe in Toth that the board abused that discretion.

# MOTION COURT: PETITIONS AND PROTECTION FROM ABUSE CASES

The next place to take my Great-Grandchildren and those curious people who are following along, is Motion Court. There is nothing else like it. If you ever have a day to watch a lower court judge in action, visit him or her in Motion Court (also known as Miscellaneous Court). Be careful not to raise your arm and hand, or suddenly stand up. The judge, in the almost always-full courtroom may call you up to the bench, believing that you have a Petition or Motion for him to handle. It is not only lawyers who appear.

But it is the lawyers' work that I tried to take up first. Their clients are usually paying by the hour. The Bar Association appreciated my effort. However, I did hear some mumblings when I announced that out-of-county attorneys would be heard first. They were our guests, and had traveled to and back from Lehigh County, thus creating more expense for their clients. Attorneys were to make their requests, usually for my signature on some or other document, when recognized by me, according to their seniority at the Bar. When two lawyers were close in seniority, I let them figure it out. On relatively few occasions, an individual came to court without counsel. Those normally called for extra patience, with the judge trying to be helpful, but not acting as the person's attorney.

There were petitions for a name change; for a continuance of a case; for permission to withdraw from a case; for a Hearing; for returning property taken by the Sheriff in a criminal matter that had resulted in an acquittal (in one case a gun!); for alternative service of notices by advertisement to persons not found; for the setting of bail; for requiring the filing of an Account; for a new trial; for ordering the production and delivery of an expert's opinion; for a Stay of a Sheriff's Sale; for approval of an individual to renew a private detective license, and many more.

Sometimes the petitioner was required to give notice to other parties so that they could be heard and perhaps contest the request. I tried to put those at the end of the list. The real end of the list was quite often a string of Protection From Abuse cases. Those all resulted in the taking of testimony. In some, the allegedly abused wanted a Court Order affording whatever protection it might offer. In others, I was requested by the abused person to release a defendant from a prior Abuse Order. The point is that a trial judge must be fairly adaptable.

Protection From Abuse cases gave me, and I think most of the judges, a real headache. For example, Judge Mellenberg, a very close friend, did not agree with me on a key issue. He was willing to issue a restraining order and permit a couple to continue to live in the same household. My position was that if the complaining spouse was in fear of bodily harm, she or he not only lost credibility on that point, but it was unfair to the police who were the ones that enforced the Order. Were they to run into the house when called and then arrest and evict the Defendant who has a right to be there? They would be caught by a "He said-She said" situation. The Legal Valley Legal Services and the Women's Center, the agencies that most often helped the victim walk through the court system, soon learned of the differing views of the two of us. Over the last ten years, the annual volume of new Petitions for Protection From Abuse Orders has remained steady at between 1,300 and 1,400.

There was one Petition for Protection From Abuse case that still casts a cloud over my judicial career. I failed miserably. I am not sure about the date or even the year. I was sitting in a sixth-floor temporary courtroom. Ms. D., accompanied by an agency representative, stated that she had sometime earlier been granted a Protection From Abuse Order against her boyfriend. A few days ago, she said, he had violated that Order by visiting her and making threats against her. He was then put into the County jail. At her request, he was brought up to my courtroom by a sheriff's deputy and was standing before me, with the agency worker standing between the couple.

I believe it was the agency case worker who told me that this latest event was not the first time that the boyfriend had violated a Protection From Abuse Order, it was his seventh. I spent some time berating him, and told him that I was going to send him to jail for a substantial period for contempt of the court Order. He admitted his wrong behavior, and promised that it would not reoccur. I did not believe him, thinking that there would probably be future harassing violations.

Ms. D. then spoke again. She asked me several times not to put him in jail. She and I argued, in a father/daughter way, for several minutes. She needed him at several levels – emotionally and for financial support. She was sure that the latest jail time would be effective. There was more said than that, which I do not recall in any detail. I gave in to her plea, and after another lecture to the man, found him in contempt, imposed a fine, and directed the Sheriff to arrange his release.

A day or so later, the local newspaper reported that she had been shot and killed by him, who then took his own life. I had to continue taking those cases, and tried not to overreact—but the fear of a repeat was on my mind.

# THE HOSPITAL CASES

There are two Opinions that I hope you will take the time to read. I think that they represent my best work. They are too long to place among the mostly short Orders and Opinions through which my narrative runs. I have placed an internet address to them in the Appendix. The St. Luke's Hospital dispute was a complicated tax assessment appeal matter. The municipalities and the School District in which St. Luke's was located joined in an effort to take away the Hospital's tax-exempt status so that it would have to pay property taxes. Those taxing bodies argued that St. Luke's was not providing enough charity care under standards set by our Commonwealth's Supreme Court. I created a formula for calculating charity, which was approved by the Commonwealth Court, but limited to the St. Luke's case. The Hospital barely passed the test.

The HealthEast Adjudication did not come to me in the normal fashion. I learned that the Lehigh County Assessment Board had denied tax-exempt status to the Hospital holding company (HealthEast, Inc.), which was the parent organization of the non-profit Allentown Hospital and the Lehigh Valley Hospital Center. By statute,

**In the Emergency Room of the Sacred Heart Hospital one evening. I wanted to see who were its primary users in my audit of the charity care being given by our local hospitals. The photographer took a trick shot using a round convex mirror already in the ER to monitor attendance.**

the charitable operation of hospitals and other non-profit organizations fall under the review of the Orphans' Court. I was greatly concerned about the loss of its tax-exempt status and issued a Citation and Order requiring HealthEast and the other general hospitals located in Lehigh County to file an Accounting of the administration of their facilities.

Extensive Hearings were held. The press provided the citizens with comprehensive information, including, for the first time in Lehigh County, photographs taken in the courtroom pursuant to a Rule I promulgated. The two hospital cases propelled me into the limelight for a short time. I was asked and agreed to talk about the cases at hospital trustee gatherings locally and in Phoenix, Cleveland, and Monterey. My message was always the same. Work at being charitable, and remember that the courts will be watching. In my view, the controlling board members were not Directors, but were Trustees.

The HealthEast dispute was settled by the parties, by having the hospital donate a series of free services and a payment by the Hospital in lieu of taxes.

I also studied the charitable performance of the Muhlenberg Osteopathic Hospital and the Sacred Heart Hospital. Muhlenberg was donating all of the free care it could reasonably afford. My ultimate conclusion was, however, that Muhlenberg Hospital was no longer needed. Sacred Heart took the honors. With very little help from the Catholic Church, it was providing charitable care beyond its ability and losing money. Its inner-city location placed it in the center of the population that most needed free or subsidized health care. Sacred Heart's emergency room had become the primary care facility for downtown Allentown. All I could do was to applaud it and urge it on.

I met with the Chief Operating Officer and later with the Board of Trustees of the Good Shepherd Home. We toured the campus and chatted with some patients and staff. Good Shepherd specialized in rehabilitation work, obtaining most of its clients, the hard cases, from the other hospitals. It had no operating room. I decided that it was not a general hospital, and did not audit their finances or write an opinion. I performed the same kind of tour at the Wiley House (now KidsPeace) then in Fountain Hill. It did not fit my definition of a hospital either.

The Hospital "visitation" effort did not just involve me as the Orphans' Court Judge, but depended upon the interest and support of the office of Pennsylvania's Attorney General. Senior Deputy Larry Barth attended and contributed at every stage. He represented through his office the people's interest. Charities, which include non-profit hospitals, are created to a great extent to relieve the government of some of its obligations, and to help fill some needy purpose to a substantial and indefinite class of persons. The courts cannot accommodate all of the individual members of such groups. It is the Attorney General's office that speaks and is heard on their behalf. Larry and Jan Thwaites sat through all of the Hearings, meetings and final Arguments by the hospital attorneys. They shared ideas and M&M's. Larry long ago joined my list of friends, although his first question when I told him about my plan for this book, was in how many of my 71 appealed cases was I reversed. I think he was pleased at the answer - four.

I believed then, and continue to believe, that St. Luke's and HealthEast (now Lehigh Valley Health Network) are not sufficiently charitable. In their competition to obtain more and more market share they are operating as profit-making businesses. They use their large surpluses to buy up weak rural medical care facilities rather than meet the health needs of our community that their own studies declare are lacking. If they become for profit organizations the courts will lose the power to oversee them, as happened in our neighboring City of Easton. My hope now is that Medicare will step in and assure that they become more altruistic by reestablishing a robust Certificate of Need program and penalizing hospitals that cannot demonstrate an appropriate level of meeting their community's healthcare needs, which non-profit hospitals were long ago required to develop. A similar rule is imposed upon certain charitable trusts and foundations that are required to expend at least five percent of their annual average annual market value for charitable purposes, or pay a 100% penalty to the government in the amount that would equal the five percent rule.

I was invited to an American Hospital Association Conference in Monterey. During a panel discussion with a LARGE audience, the moderator turned to me and asked, apropos of nothing, "What is justice?" I mumbled something about it depends upon the facts, but was totally unprepared. My topic was the legal responsibilities of hospital trustees. I decided I needed some kind of answer to that question, even if there was not a good one. Webster's Collegiate Dictionary has five attempts to define justice, but they are too academic. Plato (if he ever existed) gives me a wise-sounding meaningless platitude to use as a snappy response if I am asked again. He says that justice is when somebody gets what he or she deserves.

From left to right: Michael Seislove (former Borough of Macungie Manager—now a prominent Realtor), Me, Larry Barth (Pennsylvania Senior Deputy Attorney General), with our human-powered centrifugal force machine, that hurled an eight-pound pumpkin 220.39 feet, just nine feet short of first place.

# NATURALIZATION COURT

A court that sits in Lehigh County is Naturalization Court. It was one of my favorites. Here was a lower court State judge swearing in new United States citizens. We normally naturalized about 50-60 men, women and children at one ceremony. In most cases their families were present in the courtroom. Sometimes we had flowers on the bench and after the ceremony light refreshments. The names and the nation from which they came to America were called out one at a time. These events were all scheduled for early evening, so that those coming from a distance after work could easily attend. Many times, one of the new citizens would be called on to make remarks, and that most often became the highlight. I always had a few words of welcome. I remember saying that everybody in the room came from a foreign family, unless there was an Eskimo present. There never was.

When I think about "Naturalizing" new citizens, it brings to mind the real effect that process has upon the individual just sworn in. All of a sudden, they are handed a new bundle of essential human rights and responsibilities. They probably had some of those rights in the country that they left. If they had them all, I wonder why they changed countries. Citizens from other countries can still work and reside here. My musing about the topic brought me memories of my role as a State Trial Judge in trying to protect one of our Constitution's basic rights: to vote.

In the primary elections, the voter turnout in Lehigh County varied considerably from 42.54% in 2016 to 15.69% in 2017. However, the 2016 presidential election produced 69.69% of the 236,081 registered voters. Sadly, in the 2017 November general election, only 34.26% of the 210,505 eligible voters bothered to cast a ballot.

# ELECTION DAY DUTIES

O n election days, a judge was needed to rule on whatever challenges to a person's right to vote were raised. As is the case throughout the United States, it is the County unit of government, under the direction of the State, which actually runs the event. Our six judges divided the hours of the day that the polls were open, and each took a turn for those minutes. (About two hours.) In the primary elections, the voters' turnout was normally around forty percent, while in the general election we could expect about sixty to seventy percent. The size of the vote largely depended upon what offices were being contested, the candidates, and the weather.

Sometimes an individual appeared at a polling place and was told that he or she was not eligible to vote for a given reason. Sometimes that reason was not satisfactory. The first step was to engage the opinion of the Judge of Elections, (also an elected position) right there on the spot. Those usually involved a misspelling, incorrect house number, or other inconsistency with the official Voter's Registration Ledger. The Judge of Elections, perhaps because of his own local knowledge, or in checking the voter's driver's license or other document, could decide that the defect should be corrected, and the person be permitted to cast a ballot.

If persons were denied the right to vote at the polling booths, they were told that they could immediately go to the County's Courthouse and argue their case to the County Registrar, and if that failed, there was a judge standing by to hear the matter and to make a final decision.

When I was "standing by," in my office, normally going over Opinions, I was hoping not to be called. I knew that by the time those disputes got to me, there must be a real problem. It was my practice not to handle those issues in my courtroom, or, to wear a robe. I went across the street to where the Voter's Registration Office was then housed. In every one of my voter's cases, there was a legitimate issue. On the one hand, the County employees were dedicated to following the letter of the voter's registration laws and regulations. If a change of address form was received too late, that was too bad. If the voter had forgotten to inform the County that she had gotten married and changed her name, sorry. Other people had complied with all of the requirements; it was not fair to excuse this particular person.

On the other hand, along comes this judge, whose sole purpose is to make judgments: to balance the validity of the voting system against the constitutional right of a citizen to participate in the selection of his or her representatives. As you can gather, I tended to permit the voter to vote if I believed that no fraud was occurring and that the defect could be waived.

One voting-related matter that came to me was disturbing. During an election, I discovered through an informant that the absentee ballots that had been mailed in, mostly by service men and women, and by those who were out of the country on the election date, had been fully opened prematurely. The opener thus learned the identity of the voter, and for whom he or she voted. This violation of the right to a secret ballot was really upsetting. I immediately asked the County Solicitor to please come to see me. I also asked Jan Thwaites to join us so that there would be no doubt about the contents of the meeting.

The meeting did not go well, ending with a slammed door as the County Solicitor left the jury room we were using. In brief, after presenting the facts, I received assurances that the

County would re-instruct all those who handled the absentee ballots as to the proper procedure. However, "In order to protect the integrity of the system," would I agree not to divulge the transgression? It sounded like a cover up to me, and I declined.

# A JUDGE CANNOT SAY "I DON'T KNOW"

I am enjoying my far-distant conversation with my Great-Grandchildren, trying to give them insight into my work as a trial judge, which may give them a clue or two about me as a person. In the next sentence, I state what is for me a simple truth that greatly affected my work.

A judge cannot say, "I don't know."

We must make decisions, whether or not we are sure of the facts or the law.

And, delaying a ruling for weeks or months is normally fruitless, and is unfair to the people who are waiting for justice.

I told my law clerks that we should aim for 100% certainty, but we had to be satisfied with about an 85% result. The appellate courts were there for a reason. In cases that required a burden of proof test, that was often the decider. If, for example, you did not know if the signature on a will was legitimate or not, the burden of proof by clear and convincing evidence was on the party who challenged the signature. Thus, you upheld the will. Many types of cases imposed other burdens of proof. There are varieties of burdens, the most well-known being "beyond a reasonable doubt" for criminal charges. There are no burdens in the middle of a case when there is an objection to a question or exhibit. You rule. In a Support case, do you believe the wife or the husband? You rule. The helpful burden tests come at the end of a case, not in the midst.

Not only must trial judges decide every case, they must take every case assigned to them unless a valid conflict of interest is presented. They cannot pick and choose. Further, THE COURT IS ALWAYS OPEN TO EVERYONE. As intoned by the Court Crier, "All persons having any matter before the Court shall come forward and they shall be heard." Those words are meaningful. They tell every man and woman that he or she has a personal right to be listened to by a judge. That they have the same chance as all others to express their cause is truly empowering. It makes them a part of our judicial system. Even if they do not ever come into the courtroom, they know that they have that right.

# ON LAWYERS:
# THEIR IMPORTANCE AND TEMPERAMENT

I have talked to you about the various people who worked with me as a trial judge, including law clerks, secretaries, deputy sheriffs, Court Criers, probation officers and a great many employees of the several supporting departments in the courthouse, including those in the Office of Children and Youth, Juvenile Court, Orphans' Court, Adult Probation, Court Administration, etc. What you also need to know about is the role of the lawyers.

First to remember is that unless I misbehave, I have been and will always be a lawyer. The position of a judge, being the one who decides the thorny issues that divide people, is vitally important and should be respected. The actual body under the black robe is of no more consequence than anyone else.

The trial bar is relatively small when compared to the total number of licensed attorneys. Most lawyers spend their efforts on keeping their clients out of court, particularly out of a trial court where nothing is certain. My trial experience was limited before I became a judge. The lawyers knew that, and were generally helpful. During my tenure, I was the only judge then sitting who had served the Bar Association of Lehigh County as its President. Lawyers usually spent many months and even years getting prepared for a trial, whereas I had normally studied the court file for only an hour or so. They needed me, I needed them, and we all knew it. More than that, our whole system of justice under the rule of law is dependent upon the quality and dedication to our system of justice by the legal profession.

Each attorney was unique. In a sense, they were all actors, playing to the jury or the Court. My Great-Grandchildren will not know the lawyers who practiced before me twenty years ago, but I would like to give a flavor of their characters. The first individual that pops into my mind is Richard, short, overweight, hair down to his eyebrows, with his shirt always sticking out over his belt. He did not look lawyerlike. He handled mostly family matters. But he was articulate, polite, and smart. When he spoke, we all listened. You could not judge him by his appearance.

Robert, on the other hand, was a bully. He too was sharp, but nasty and abrasive. He seemed to enjoy making caustic remarks to his opposing counsel, particularly if a younger lawyer. In one matter, I recall him not making a formal objection to a question, but blurting out, "That was a stupid question!"

When Mr. W. entered the courtroom, he attracted attention by his impeccable attire, while Attorney S. always wore a rose in his lapel that he had grown in his own greenhouse. The number of women lawyers had substantially increased since the time I was admitted to the Bar in 1956. They often took on the very difficult family cases, and provided a needed shield for their clients.

I could tell the best lawyers by the degree of preparedness when I, or opposing counsel, asked a question. I always had the feeling that the lawyers in my courtroom believed that they were doing something special, and that quiet respect was due the court and any other participants in the proceeding.

Most lawyers look like the average citizens that they are, but they do have a big responsibility to shoulder. Trial lawyers have the leading percentage of alcoholism of any other specialty, and for good reason. They are retained to resolve a dispute by trial. The defense lawyers usually are paid by the hour, but the plaintiff's counsel are often required to advance substantial sums to pay for expert witnesses, and are reimbursed and paid a fee based upon the result. The witnesses do not want to come; the Court Administrator's office is never quite sure when a judge and jury will be available; the client wants the lawyer to do the talking, and squawks at the need for his own rehearsal, and there are or are not settlement negotiations in process. Frankly, I would rather be the judge, just trying to run a fair trial.

# A TAX ASSESSMENT CASE:
# MACK TRUCKS VS. COUNTY OF LEHIGH

The next two decisions sent up on appeal to the Commonwealth Court relate to different kinds of taxes. The first concerns the value placed upon the Mack Truck World Headquarters (the assessment), the figure which is used in calculating the taxes on real estate, multiplied by the tax millage. In the Mack case, my March 28th Order with footnote was appealed. My short May 22nd (1995) Opinion is included because I needed to address what I thought was an incorrect but novel theory, a theory which was also rejected by the Commonwealth Court.

IN THE COURT OF COMMON PLEAS OF LEHIGH COUNTY, PENNSYLVANIA

CIVIL ACTION - LAW

MACK TRUCKS, INC.,                 )
                                   )
                Petitioner         )
                                   )
        vs.                        )
                                   )
LEHIGH COUNTY BOARD OF             )
ASSESSMENT APPEALS,                )
                                   )  No. 93-C-2539
                Respondent         )
                                   )
        and                        )
                                   )
COUNTY OF LEHIGH,                  )
                                   )
                Intervenor         )

\*     \*     \*     \*     \*

APPEARANCES:

> ANTHONY R. THOMPSON, ESQUIRE,
> And with him, THOMPSON, SOMACH & VanGILDER,
>    On behalf of Mack Trucks, Inc.

> EMIL W. KANTRA, II, ESQUIRE,
> and with him, HONORABLE MADALINE PALLADINO,
> Lehigh County Solicitor,
>    On behalf of Lehigh County.

\*     \*     \*     \*     \*

## OPINION

ROBERT K. YOUNG, Judge.

The Court determined by its Order of March 28,

1995 that the fair market value of the Mack Truck World Headquarters for real estate tax purposes for the years 1993 and 1994 was the sum of $7,500,000. The factual basis for that decision and the reasons adopted by the Court were set forth in a footnote to that Order which is incorporated by this reference as the Court's Opinion.

Following an appeal to the Commonwealth Court by the County of Lehigh, the Court was provided, pursuant to a Rule 1925(b) Order, with the County's Statement of Matters Complained of on Appeal. Three reasons for the Appeal have been provided.

As to the first reason, the County differs with the factual determination made by the Trial Court that the highest and best use for the World Headquarters on the open market is as a rehabilitated multi-use facility. The footnote to the March 28, 1995 Order addresses that issue.

The second matter complained of is the Trial Court's determination that the fair market value was set at $7,500,000. The County thus objects to the Court's final conclusion, which is why it has appealed. As to that "precise reason", the footnote must speak for itself.

The last matter complained of is a puzzle. The

-2-

County of Lehigh argues that in setting the fair market value of the property, the present owner, Mack Trucks, should be considered a potential buyer. It already owns the property. If the definition of fair market value is the price a willing buyer would sell a property to a willing seller, neither party being compelled to enter into such an agreement, how can one negotiate with oneself. The Trial Court does not understand the County's position on this issue, and it is not able to address it in this Opinion, except to find as a fact that if Mack Trucks decided to sell the property to itself it would most likely convert the building for use by multi-tenants. As noted in the footnote, this is, in essence, what Bethlehem Steel did with its World Headquarters, which is a much larger facility also located in Lehigh County.

BY THE COURT:

Robert K. Young, J.

Dated: May 22 , 1995.

-3-

IN THE COURT OF COMMON PLEAS OF LEHIGH COUNTY, PENNSYLVANIA

CIVIL ACTION - LAW

MACK TRUCKS, INC.,                          )
                                            )
          Petitioner                        )
                                            )
     vs.                                    )
                                            )
LEHIGH COUNTY BOARD OF                      )
ASSESSMENT APPEALS,                         )
                                            )   No. 93-C-2539
          Respondent                        )
                                            )
     and                                    )
                                            )
COUNTY OF LEHIGH,                           )
                                            )
          Intervenor                        )

## ORDER

NOW, this *18th* day of March, 1995, following
a Hearing, the entry of written Briefs and oral Argument,

IT IS ORDERED that the market value of the real
property located at 2100 Mack Boulevard, Allentown, Lehigh
County (Tax Parcel No. 0219H09SE4006005) is hereby
established as of September 1, 1993 and as of September 1,
1994 at $7,500,000.00.[1]

BY THE COURT:

Robert K. Young, Judge

(Footnote on next page)

[1]The key factual issue in this case is whether the highest and best use for the subject premises in the present real estate market in Lehigh County is as a facility for a single user, or as rehabilitated multi-user tenant-occupied property. That is, is it reasonably probable that if put on the market, the 227,400 square foot World Headquarters complex would be sold to an entity which would use it for that new buyer's own purposes, or, is the most likely purchaser one who would convert the buildings for use by a variety of tenants.

The Court is of the opinion that it is highly improbable that a single user could be found for what is an extremely inefficient structure. The Lehigh Valley (and most of the United States) is experiencing a major shift away from conspicuous image-building construction, to a more cost-effective use of corporate resources. The world headquarters was erected in a different era. The most striking deficiency is the heating and air conditioning system. The electrically fueled heating boilers consume an extraordinary amount of energy. The actual heat for the occupants comes from metal plates in the ceilings. The total cost of electricity (including all uses except the computer room) is the highest of any commercial customer in the Lehigh Valley. The average electric bill over the years 1992-1994 is $922,000.00 per year. There are extravagant uses of space within the building, particularly the first floor entrance/showroom, the cafeteria, and the auditorium.

There is adequate land for landscaping and parking (22.3089 acres). However, the location and neighborhood is rather neutral for an entity of the size that would be interested in making such a large purchase. Access to I-78 and Route 309 is excellent, but the tract is surrounded by a mix of industrial, commercial and residential uses. The property is in the flight path of the Queen City Airport's most active runway. The location is not bad, but in order to attract the kind of purchaser who intends to keep the basic structure and utilize the building for its own purposes, the location needs to be appealing which it is not.

In addition to the property's structural inefficiencies and plain location, there are very few customers looking for a 227,000 square foot six-story facility. Bethlehem Steel was not able to sell its headquarters building, and has elected to rent most of the space to others. It took CertainTeed two years to market its headquarters building in Montgomery

CONTINUATION OF· FOOTNOTE
_____

County, which has been renovated and sublet.   In short, and
as noted ·by Del C. Markward, a realtor specializing in large
commercial buildings for the Jackson-Cross Company, the odds
of finding a single-purpose purchaser for the Mack World
Headquarters building are one in a hundred.   Such a chance
is not "reasonably probable".   The highest and best use is,
therefore, for rehabilitation, renovation,and renting to
multiple tenants.

*   *   *   *   *

The professional expert appraisers presented their opinions
regarding the value which should be ascribed to the property
if the Court would find that multiple tenants is its best
use.  Appraiser John J. Coyle performed a detailed analysis
of the real estate market, the cost of rehabilitating the
property, the financial returns expected, and comparable
projects.  Using the three recognized traditional approaches
to valuation of real·estate, he opined that a willing buyer
would pay $6,900,000.00 for the premises.   Mr. Del C.
Markward used his extensive experience in preparing a
similar report, and testified that if purchased for retrofit
to be rented to multiple tenants, the fair market value
would be "somewhere in the $10.00 to $20.00 per square foot
range, depending on the scope of modifications necessary to
bring the building up to market standards."   At 250,000
gross square feet, his opinion of market value is,
therefore, $2,500,000.00 to $5,000,000.00.   Deborah S.
Skeans, another well-qualified appraiser, is of the belief
that a single user could be found, and on that basis placed
the fair market value at $10,500,000.00.

The profession of appraising real estate is not a science,
nor is the law.   Elements of experience and judgment are
required.  Objective evidence is often lacking.  The Courts
have long held that parcels of realty by their nature are
unique.  The Court must, therefore, use whatever evidence is
at hand, and then make what must be a somewhat subjective
decision.  Perhaps that one-in-a-hundred buyer may appear,
and may like the property the way it is now configured
(except for the heating system).  However, the Court is of
the opinion that the fair market value will reflect the
substantial costs of rehabilitating the building, and that
because of the cost of borrowing those funds and the

-3-

CONTINUATION OF FOOTNOTE

---

necessary delay in finding suitable tenants at that location in the City of Allentown, a fair market price would be $7,500,000.00.

# HAB INDUSTRIES VS. CITY OF ALLENTOWN: BUSINESS PRIVILEGE TAX ON MANUFACTURING, OR WAS IT PROCESSING?

A tax of another sort that came before me was the Business Privilege Tax imposed by the City of Allentown (and elsewhere). The footnote Opinion to the next case is not written as seriously minded as was usual for me. I was having a little fun with the legislature and appellate court. If you take the 1993 challenge test I made, my guess is that you will not score 100%. Yes, I was affirmed.

IN THE COURT OF COMMON PLEAS OF LEHIGH COUNTY, PENNSYLVANIA

CIVIL ACTION - LAW

HAB INDUSTRIES, INC.,          )
                               )
          Petitioner           )
                               )
     vs.                       )    No. 90-C-1325
                               )
CITY OF ALLENTOWN,             )
                               )
          Respondent           )

ORDER

NOW, this *2nd* day of *July*, 1993, following a full Hearing, the entry of written Briefs and oral Argument,

IT IS ORDERED that the Petition for Review of HAB Industries, Inc., claiming an exemption from the Respondent City of Allentown's Business Privilege Tax, is Denied.[1]

IT IS FURTHER ORDERED that the Petitioner, HAB Industries, Inc., is engaged in a "service" business, and is subject to a rate of three (3) mills under the City of Allentown's Business Privilege Tax.[2]

BY THE COURT:

Robert K. Young, Judge

(Footnote on next page)

---

[1]The Local Tax Enabling Act, 53 P.S. §6901, et seq. sets forth those activities which may be taxed by local political subdivisions. Pennsylvania's Cities, Townships, and Boroughs are not authorized to tax the enterprise of "manufacturing". The stated purpose of that exemption is to foster industry competitive with other states. They are, however, permitted to exact revenue for "processing".

The courts have been obligated to define the difference between these two undertakings, and over the years the distinction has become blurred, although the consequences of the difference are substantial. For example, we challenge the reader to decide correctly whether the following examples are manufacturing or processing. The legal answers will be provided later.

> (1) A raw potato is cleaned, skinned, cut into slivers, cooked in oil, salted, put into a bag, and sent to others to sell as potato chips. Manufacturing or processing?

> (2) A collector of raw honey, unfit for human consumption, pasteurizes and filters it, and packages it for retail sale.

> (3) A bookbinder receives large flat sheets of paper which are already printed, cuts them, puts them in sequence, pastes them, binds them, and returns them to the printer.

> (4) A company produces diesel engines by acquiring used engine blocks, breaking them down, salvaging some of the parts, and combining them with more new parts than old ones to make usable engines.

> (5) Turning milk into cottage cheese and ice cream.

-2-

CONTINUATION OF FOOTNOTE

---

(6) Mixing pressurized air with water to create artificial snow.

The appellate courts distinguish manufacturing from processing by examining the end product. That is, if the taxpayer's activities result in a fundamental change in the form, composition, or character of whatever item is being handled, such a taxpayer is a manufacturer. On the other hand, if there is no change in the form, composition or character of the goods, the taxpayer is engaged in "processing".

The term manufacturing, as used in the exemption provision of the Local Tax Enabling Act involves the concept of transforming materials or things "into something different from that received. The difference cannot be a superficial change that does not alter or change the thing ... what is required is that the basic materials or goods be given a new identity by the current producer, one which can be easily traced to such producer ... when labor is used ... to produce a different product than the original, one with a new identify, manufacturing has occurred." Bindex Corp. v. City of Pittsburgh, 504 Pa. 584, 587, 475 A.2d 1320, 1322 (1984).

The facts of this case have been stipulated. In essence, the taxpayer is a "converter" of raw cloth. It bleaches, scours, dyes, prints, bulks, naps, slits, cuts, tenters, resinates, calendars, gums, stretches, cures, heat sets, mildew proofs, permanently presses, adds dimensional stability and provides flame retardants and water repellants to otherwise unusable "greige" goods. It takes newly made fabric as it comes from the knitter and "finishes" the material, so that it can be made into clothing and other useful items. The work done by the taxpayer greatly enhances the value of the product. The unrefuted testimony indicated that on average, the treatment of the raw cloth by the converter adds between $4.00 - $8.00 per pound to the value of the greige goods, which initially cost approximately $2.00 per pound.

-3-

CONTINUATION OF FOOTNOTE

---

The converter does not own the cloth at any stage, but is merely treating it on a commission basis. After the cloth has been treated, it is sent on to others for final finishing into curtains, clothing, linens, etc. In order to perform its work, the converter must add several types of chemicals in differing amounts in specific sequence. It is clear that skill and labor are necessary.

However, as was noted in City of Reading v. Forty-five Noble Street, Inc., 50 Pa. Cmmw. 431, 413 A.2d 1153 (1980), the taxpayer started with cloth and ended up with cloth, not a new and different article. The City of Reading case is directly on point, and although there may be economic reasons for a tax change, such must be accomplished by the legislature, not by a trial court. See also, Tax Review Board of the City of Philadelphia v. Keystone Dyeing Co., Inc., 26 Pa. Cmmw. 524, 364 A.2d 749 (1976). In 1971, the legislature did reform provisions of the Sales and Use Tax (72 Pa.C.S.A. §7101 et.seq.) and provided specific definitions of both "manufacture" and "processing". These terms were again defined in a 1991 amendment to that Act. At Section 7201 (d) (2), processing is now defined, among others, as the "scouring, carbonizing, cording, combing, throwing, twisting or winding of natural or synthetic fibers, or the spinning, bleaching, dyeing, printing or finishing of yarns or fabrics, when such activities are performed prior to sale to the ultimate consumer." Thus, although it appears that reasonable minds could differ with the variety of holdings as to what is and what is not manufacturing, both the appellate courts and the legislature have decided that the treatment of greige goods by a converter is processing and, therefore, can be taxed under the Local Tax Enabling Act.

[2]Again, see Tax Review Board of the City of Philadelphia v. Keystone Dyeing Co., Inc., supra, wherein it was held that a comparable dyeing and finishing company, which owned no inventory, was engaged in a "service" enterprise.

\* \* \* \* \*

-4-

CONTINUATION OF FOOTNOTE

_____

Answers:

(1)  Potato case, Commonwealth v. Snyder's Bakery, 348 Pa. 308, 35 A.2d 260 (1944), manufacturing;

(2)  Honey,  Steward Honeybee Products, Inc. v. Commonwealth, Board of Finance & Revenue, 525 Pa. 222, 579 A.2d 872 (1990), processing;

(3)  Bookbinder,  Bindex  Corp.  v.  City  of Pittsburgh,  504  Pa.  584,  475  A.2d  1320  (1984), manufacturing;

(4)  Re-manufactured engines, Mack Truck. Inc. v. Commonwealth of Pennsylvania, No. 207 F.R. 1989, dated June 11, 1993 (Opinion not reported), processing;

(5)  Milk  into  ice  cream  and  cottage cheese, Rieck-McJunkin Dairy Co. v. School District of Pittsburgh, 362 Pa. 13, 66 A.2d 295 (1949), manufacturing; and

(6)  Artificial  snow,  Ski  Roundtop,  Inc.  v. Commonwealth,  520  Pa.  227,  553  A.2d  928  (1989), manufacturing.

# TOLL BROTHERS, INC. VS. SOUTH WHITEHALL TOWNSHIP

The methods used to extract our money by the various governmental bodies that have jurisdiction over us are myriad. When my friends talk about taxes, they are mostly complaining about income taxes, real estate taxes, sales taxes and gasoline taxes. We just looked at the Mack real estate tax assessment dispute and the H. A. B. Business Privilege Tax. The next Opinion required me to examine the legality and fairness of yet another source of revenue for a local Township: Not a tax, but a fee.

IN THE COURT OF COMMON PLEAS OF LEHIGH COUNTY, PENNSYLVANIA

CIVIL ACTION - MANDAMUS

TOLL BROTHERS, INC.,        )
             Plaintiff     )
                           )
     vs.                   )
                           )      NO. 89-C-299
BOARD OF COMMISSIONERS OF   )
SOUTH WHITEHALL TOWNSHIP,    )
LEHIGH COUNTY,              )
             Defendant      )

*     *     *     *     *

APPEARANCES:

        JOSEPH A. FITZPATRICK, ESQUIRE,
        DONNA M. MILLER, ESQUIRE,
        And with them, FITZPATRICK, LENTZ & BUBBA,
           On behalf of the Plaintiff.

        DAVID G. KNERR, ESQUIRE
        BLAKE C. MARLES, ESQUIRE,
        And with them, WEAVER, MOSEBACH, PIOSA,
        HIXSON, WALLITSCH & MARLES,
           On behalf of the Defendant.

*     *     *     *     *

OPINION

ROBERT K. YOUNG, Judge.

    In  1987-88,  the  Defendant  Township  (South
Whitehall) gave Final Plan Approval to the Plaintiff (Toll
Brothers) for the construction of eighty-four (84) homes in
two subdivisions.  Toll Brothers immediately applied for and

received nine (9) construction permits for the initial phase of the development of this project.  Each of these permits cost the Plaintiff $500.00.  That fee was in effect before and after South Whitehall approved Toll Brothers' final plans, and was in exchange for permission to connect to the Township's public water and sewer lines.  Shortly after granting Final Approval and after issuing the above-noted 9 permits, South Whitehall, on December 6, 1988, passed a new ordinance requiring $4,000.00 for each construction permit as the connection fee.  This was an 800% increase.  In order to continue the projects, Toll Brothers paid these extra costs, under protest.  That protest has taken the form of this lawsuit, seeking a Court Order requiring the return of $3,500.00 per construction permit it had to pay after South Whitehall raised the connection fee.

Following the entry of written Briefs and oral Argument, the Trial Court entered an Order on November 7, 1990 directing South Whitehall to refund any monies paid for the relevant permits in excess of $500.00.  That Order is the subject of an appeal to the Commonwealth Court of Pennsylvania, which necessitates this Opinion.

South Whitehall has specified three issues in its

-2-

Statement of Matters Complained of on Appeal. The first is that Mandamus is not the appropriate remedy in this case. South Whitehall argues that Toll Brothers is not seeking to have the Township issue permits for the seventy-five (75) remaining lots (this has already been done), but rather seeks to have what it claims is the excess money returned. It is clear that this is the relief sought by the Plaintiff in its Complaint, in its Amended Complaint, and in its two briefs filed in this matter.

South Whitehall filed Preliminary Objections to the initial Complaint. There was one objection, in the nature of a demurrer to Toll Brothers' request for attorney's fees. That was the **ONLY** objection raised. Pa.R.C.P. No. 1028(b) states that "[a]ll preliminary objections shall be raised at one time." The Township preliminarily objected in the nature of a demurrer under Pa.R.C.P. No. 1017(b)(4), but did not include a motion to strike any pleadings because of a lack of conformity to law or rule of court under Pa.R.C.P. No. 1017(b)(2), nor did the Township raise the issue of Mandamus when the Plaintiff filed an Amended Complaint. Instead, South Whitehall executed a Stipulation of Counsel closing the pleadings, and only thereafter noted its

-3-

objection to the Mandamus nature of these proceedings.

There appears to be little difference between requesting a Court to compel the ministerial act of issuing a permit, or to compel a refund due on the overpayment of a permit. In any event, the Township can show no prejudice, and has by its inaction waived any objection to the use by Toll Brothers of the Mandamus procedure.

The second matter complained of on appeal is that 53 P.S. §10508(4) does not prohibit South Whitehall from increasing connection fees during a five year period after the final approval of the Plaintiff's development plan. 53 P.S. §10508(4)(ii) states in part:

> (4) Changes in the ordinance shall affect plats as follows:...
> (ii) When an application for approval of a plat ... has been approved ...., no subsequent change or amendment in the zoning, subdivision or other governing ordinance or plan shall be applied to affect adversely the right of the applicant to commence and to complete any aspect of the approved development in accordance with the terms of such approval within five years from such approval.

The Township contends that its increase in the cost of water and sewer connection fees did not affect the Plaintiff's

-4-

right to develop the property. The Plaintiff is still allowed to develop the approved plan, after paying the $3,500.00 per lot boost in connection fees for each construction permit. However, without these connections, (which are made at the sole expense of Toll Brothers), the Plaintiff cannot effectuate the planned development previously approved by the Township. Sewer and water connections are two aspects of the approved plan. It is clear that an 800% increase in the cost of making those connections adversely affects the Plaintiff's financial ability to commence and complete the entire project, in violation of the above-noted Act.

Any charge increase of such magnitude following final approval of the development is patently unfair. Yet, a municipality should not be forever holden to approval costs made in the distant past. The five-year time period of the statute clearly strikes the proper balance. It prevents land developers from obtaining permission to build and then sitting on that approval for too long a time. However, it also prevents a municipality from changing its ordinances in such a way that the right to develop according to an approved plan becomes meaningless. Under 53 P.S.

-5-

10508(4)(ii) Toll Brothers was entitled to effectuate the approved development plan for a period of five years under the ordinances as they existed at the time of the approval. Therefore, the proper sewer and water connection fees which Toll Brothers owed to South Whitehall were $500.00, not $4,000.00, and the Township is obligated to return the difference.

We are unsure of the significance of the third matter complained of on appeal, which states:  "[t]he South Whitehall Township sewer and water connection fees are not merely 'inspection' fees".  This is in reference to a parenthetical statement to the contrary made by the Trial Court in its footnote Order of November 7, 1990.

It is the Court's understanding after hearing oral Argument that in South Whitehall Township the developer is required to perform all of the work involved in making connections to the existing Township water and sewer lines. The Township Engineer must inspect and approve the work before the trench can be closed.  The Court presumes that something was done by the Township in exchange for the $42,000.00 it is to be paid for the 84 lots at $500.00 each.

Had not the legislature wisely provided a five-year

-6-

stay on increasing the burdens upon a developer after final plan approval, South Whitehall's coffers would have gained an additional $262,500.00 for doing nothing extra.

Robert K. Young, Judge

Dated: 4/15/95

# SLIP AND FALL:
# HOLLY KOHLER VS. HERBERT HYMAN

M oving from tax cases, and keeping up my effort to provide the kind of variety that was intriguing to me, the following two cases deal with liability in "slip-and-fall" events. There were quite a few of these, where people fell on sidewalk ice, wet floors in shopping stores and almost anywhere where the terrain is uneven. The owners of the property are not automatically liable. The plaintiff must establish negligence, and the duty of care of property owners depends upon the use of the premises. A patron in a store, whose attention is normally on the merchandise, is entitled to have the aisles kept clear, whereas a trespasser by law assumes a degree of risk.

IN THE COURT OF COMMON PLEAS OF LEHIGH COUNTY, PENNSYLVANIA

CIVIL DIVISION

| | | |
|---|---|---|
| HOLLY KOHLER and JOSEPH KOHLER, Husband and Wife, | ) ) ) | |
| Plaintiffs | ) ) | |
| vs. | ) ) | No. 1986-C-1809 |
| HERBERT HYMAN and CLAYTON HYMAN, | ) ) ) | |
| Defendants | ) ) | |

\*    \*    \*    \*    \*

APPEARANCES:

        GEORGE HEITCZMAN, ESQUIRE,
        And with him, O'HARE & HEITCZMAN,
           On behalf of the Plaintiffs.

        MARK S. SIGMON, ESQUIRE,
        And with him, SIGMON & SIGMON,
           On behalf of the Defendants.

\*    \*    \*    \*    \*

OPINION

ROBERT K. YOUNG, Judge.

This matter involves what is commonly called a "slip and fall" case. However, rather than dealing with rough or icy surfaces, the Plaintiffs' allegations are that the fall occurred because the Defendant property owners failed to provide a stair handrail of sufficient length. The issues were tried by a jury, which found that the Defendants were not negligent. The Plaintiffs seek a judgment notwithstanding the verdict or, in the alternative, a new trial. On June 12, 1990, this Court denied those Motions. Plaintiffs have appealed that Order, thus requiring this Opinion.

On November 18, 1984, Plaintiff Holly Kohler (Holly) picked up a plastic wash basket full of laundry and stepped out onto the small landing in front of her apartment. She was wearing one-month old shoes known as "flats", which are connected to the foot by a strap in the front which fits between the big and second toe. The weather had been cold and drizzling, and she carefully slid her shoe lightly sidewise to be certain that the surface of the landing was not slick. It was not. She proceeded down a few steps onto a sloping walkway which led across the front yard to a second set of cement steps. She reached those steps without incident and continued on to descend the final steps which would put her at the parking lot level of the common laundry room where she intended to wash her clothes.

Holding the wash basket with both hands to one

side, Holly moved forward and down the last flight of seven steps. When she reached the last step she started to slip. She grabbed for the stair railing but could not reach it because it did not extend to her side. Her foot caught between the curb and a rolled macadam car barrier. She fell and severely broke her ankle. The crux of the case against the Defendants is that the stair railing did not extend all the way down to the bottom parking lot level. The photographic exhibits are helpful in depicting the scene of this accident. Exhibit P-2 is attached hereto.

Holly had used these stairs many times before (although she usually cut across the lawn to get to the laundry room). She testified that she did not use the handrail for the first six steps, as both of her hands were holding onto the wash basket. It was her opinion, however, that as she fell, she threw the basket down and could have stopped her fall by grabbing onto the handrail if it had been there.

Each party called an expert witness. The Plaintiffs' expert indicated that when the property was constructed (several years earlier by prior owners), it should have been built with a handrail extending down to the final level. The 1970 BOCA Code was cited to the jury for that proposition. The Defendants' expert expressed the opinion that the BOCA Code was not applicable, because the Plaintiff did not fall on a stairway, but rather on a landing. He explained the difference to the jury, analyzing the outside steps at the apartment complex to those outside of the courthouse, requiring no handrail. Both experts were well qualified. The Plaintiffs' counsel did not challenge the Defendants' expert as to his credentials.

Thus, the jury was not faced with any particularly difficult factual issue. Holly's version of what happened was not seriously contested. The main issue was whether or not the construction of the handrail was negligent. The experts disagreed, and the jury filled out the Verdict Slip by answering in the negative only the question of the Defendants' negligence. They did not reach the issue of whether Holly was contributively negligent. Therefore, the jury must have found the Defendants' expert more credible than the Plaintiffs'.

The trial court's decision to let the case go to the jury is the subject of this appeal. In the Concise Statement of Matters Complained of on Appeal, the Plaintiffs first state that the Court should have granted binding instructions in favor of Plaintiffs both under the law and

-4-

under the facts. The Plaintiffs argue that as a matter of law the Defendants were negligent as the owners of a property on which outside steps were located with a handrail that did not extend to the bottom level. The Plaintiffs have not provided any reason for such a position. The only proposition that is apparent in declaring absolute liability in this case would be that the construction of the handrail was in violation of the BOCA Code, which code was adopted by reference by an ordinance of the City of Allentown.

The trial court charged the jury that Allentown did have such an ordinance in effect at the time the handrail was constructed. The jury was instructed that if they found that the ordinance was violated that that would be some evidence of negligence, but not negligence per se. (N. T. pp. 234, 235). Such is the law of Pennsylvania as per Murphy v. Bernheim & Sons, Inc., 327 Pa. 285, 293, 194 A. 194, 197 (1937). See also, Wisniewski v. Chestnut Hill Hospital, 403 Pa. 610, 611-12, 170 A.2d 595, 596 (and cases cited herein) (1961).

Plaintiffs seek a new trial on two grounds. First, because the trial judge refused the two following points for charge:

-5-

4. You are instructed that because the steps on which Mrs. Kohler fell were exposed to the weather and it was therefore foreseeable that they could become slippery, the Defendants had a duty as a matter of law to equip the stairway with a graspable handrail or some other device that would have offered her refuge when she lost her footing. _Kuminkoski v. Daum_, 429 Pa. 494, 240 A.2d 524 (1968).

5. If you find that the handrail did not extend to the portion of the steps where Mrs. Kohler fell, then you must find that Defendants breached their duty to provide a graspable handrail or other device to offer her a refuge. _Kuminkoski v. Daum_, 429 Pa. 494, 240 A.2d 524 (1968).

It should initially be noted that the _Kuminkoski_ decision was authored in 1968 by Justice Musmanno, with three dissents. In that case the jury was deadlocked. The jury was discharged and the trial judge entered a judgment in favor of the Defendant. It was a slip and fall case, on steps, and the Supreme Court merely held that the Plaintiff was entitled to a new trial before another jury. There was evidence that the Defendants had continuously spread sawdust upon the steps, which often became wet and slippery. Thus, the issue was not clear enough to be decided as a matter of law. In the case at bar the jury was instructed that the landlord had a duty to use ordinary care to avoid injury to

-6-

others. The jury was more specifically charged as follows:

> The duty was there, and if you sought to find there was some cause then between the breach of that duty and the injuries, and if you find that the defendant had a duty, in this case to Mrs. Kohler, to provide a handrail, or other device, to offer her a refuge, when and where she fell, then you would find the defendants were negligent. If you find they had that duty, then you've got that negligence. You are instructed that the defendants had a duty to provide adequate light on the stairs.
>
> Now the landlord of a multi-resident building, this is some law from other cases. The landlord of a multi-residential building, who has control of a common walkway, or approachway, has a duty to keep said walkway, or approachway, reasonably safe for its tennants (sic). And this duty may extend beyond the requirements of a code or ordinance.

In light of the differing expert opinions, it would have been inappropriate for the Court to have declared that as a matter of law the existing handrail constituted negligence.

The second reason given for the request for a new trial is the trial court's refusal to permit the Plaintiffs' expert, in this Civil case, to state his opinion that the failure to provide an extended handrail was negligence.

-7-

This ruling was made upon the basis of <u>Ryan v. Furey</u>, 225 Pa. Super. 294, 303 A.2d 221 (1973).  See also <u>Com. v. Samuels</u>, 354 Pa. 128, 138, 511 A.2d. 221 (1986).  This was not a complex nor technical happening.  The case was well tried in less than two days.  The jury was the proper body to make the decision as to whether or not the Defendants were negligent in safely maintaining their property.  The facts were sufficiently developed at the trial to enable the jury to arrive at its ultimate verdict without the expert's opinion on that conclusive issue.

BY THE COURT:

Robert K. Young, Judge

Dated: August 13, 1990

# MEDICAL MALPRACTICE:
# THE HIGH/LOW CONCEPT

If a person is injured in any manner, as was Holly in the preceding case, the first step is to obtain the services of a medical doctor. The results of the treatment by the doctor are not always satisfactory, which leads me now into the work done as a trial judge in medical malpractice cases. I cannot accurately recall how many of these lawsuits were assigned to me over the period I was a judge, but at least a dozen. There was always one hanging over my trial schedule. They take a long time and are a challenge.

The attorneys in medical malpractice disputes were generally very smart, well prepared, imaginative, and to an extent, aggressive. Those attributes are required by the defending doctor's insurance company and by lawyers representing injured Plaintiffs. There was a great deal at stake. In serious cases, the plaintiff had either died or was facing long-term or permanent pain or disfigurement. A finding of negligence against the doctor affected his ability to obtain referrals; diminished his stature among his peers; resulted in loss of hospital privileges, and provided embarrassment.

Many malpractice cases were settled. Depending upon the terms of the doctor's insurance policy, it was not unusual for a physician to refuse to settle. Briefly, regarding settlement of all cases, there were in my time some novel legal ideas in vogue. The most popular was known as "High and Low". The bargain was that the case would go to trial, and whatever the jury or judge awarded, the plaintiff would receive at least an agreed sum (let's say $250,000), but not more than, for example, $500,000. Thus, the defendant had a cap on the damages, while the plaintiff would at least be protected by an acceptable minimum sum.

The high/low concept worked well when the main issue was the amount of compensation such as loss of future earnings, worth of past and future pain and suffering, degree of disfigurement, etc. If the liability of the doctor was the sticking point, it was sometimes agreed that the case would be bifurcated. That is, the fact finder (jury or judge) would only be asked to determine whether or not there was medical negligence, and whether that negligence was the proximate cause of the plaintiff's injuries. That system avoided the costly process of calling expensive expert witnesses regarding the damages aspects if no negligence was found—the case was over. If there was causative negligence, the damage issue was usually settled because then neither side wanted to risk the jury setting the amount. I felt that I had an important role in promoting settlements, but tried to remain neutral and not force the parties together. Judge Larry Brenner was noted to have a very high ratio of settlements, much higher than mine.

The Moses medical malpractice litigation will acquaint you with both procedural and evidentiary issues that often pop up in the middle of that type of dispute. I am presenting the short factual Memorandum handed down by the Superior Court. My footnote is at the end. As soon as the witnesses have all testified and the closing summaries of the parties are over, the jury is "charged" with a series of "points for charge" by the judge. This is the way that the jury receives the laws that relate to each particular case. I could usually prepare most of those points during the recesses or before or after the trial started, but depending upon what testimony was actually put before the jury, there is often a need to add or delete some points. Because the jury is waiting, there is some pressure on the judge.

My habit was to call a recess for the jury and ask the lawyers to come up to the bench to go over my charge, and the separate points for charge which they wanted me to tell the jury: a so-called "sidebar."  Most of those charges had been standardized in a huge three-binder book, but "one size did not fit all." It was necessary to delete some that were not applicable and to modify others. Sometimes when I thought those points were a bit awkward or confusing, I took a chance at simplifying them.

In the Moses case, I did not remove Dr. Dickson's name from the case due to the fact that he was exonerated by the jury.

J. S20020/95

MARIO F. MOSES AND MITRI MOSES, : IN THE SUPERIOR COURT OF
                    Appellant    :      PENNSYLVANIA
                                 :
        v.                       :
                                 :
THOMAS B. DICKSON, M.D., AND     :
ORTHOPAEDIC ASSOCIATES OF        :
ALLENTOWN, INC.,                 :
                    Appellees    :   NO. 04362 PHL 1994


Appeal from the Judgment entered May 4, 1995 in
the Court of Common Pleas of Lehigh County, Civil
No. 87-C-2850


BEFORE:   HUDOCK, SAYLOR, AND HESTER, JJ.


MEMORANDUM:

FILED JUL - 5 1995

This is an appeal from an order of the Court of Common
Pleas of Lehigh County entering judgment on a jury verdict in
favor of Appellees, Thomas B. Dickson, M.D., and Orthopaedic
Associates of Allentown, Inc. ("Orthopaedic Associates"), in
a medical malpractice action. We affirm.

Appellant, Mario Moses, twisted his back during
wrestling practice in December of 1993 and was treated by the
school trainer. Later in the month, Moses again experienced
extreme back pain and had trouble moving his left leg.
Moses' father took him to the hospital where x-rays were
taken. The hospital's emergency room physician gave Moses a
prescription and instructed him to rest. In January 1984,
Moses consulted Dr. Dickson concerning pain in his lower
back. Following an examination, Dr. Dickson advised Moses

141

that he had a torn paraspinous muscle and prescribed physical therapy. In rendering his diagnosis, Dr. Dickson did not personally review the x-ray films which had been taken at the hospital, but relied upon a radiologist's report which indicated that the x-rays were negative for a fracture. Following physical therapy, Moses seemed to improve. In October of 1984, Moses again consulted Dr. Dickson due to lower back pain which again diminished following physical therapy. In December 1985, Moses returned to Dr. Dickson complaining of lower back pain. Dr. Dickson ordered x-rays and scheduled a bone scan. The tests revealed that Moses had a fractured vertebra, and Dr. Dickson prescribed the use of a back brace for three months. Moses then consulted another physician, Dr Mark Cerciello, and discontinued his treatment with Dr. Dickson.

IN THE COURT OF COMMON PLEAS OF LEHIGH COUNTY, PENNSYLVANIA

CIVIL ACTION - LAW

MARIO F. MOSES and )
MITRI MOSES, )
)
      Plaintiff )
)
      vs. )   No. 87-C-2850
)
THOMAS B. DICKSON, M.D., )
and ORTHOPAEDIC ASSOCIATES )
OF ALLENTOWN, INC., )
)
      Defendants )

## ORDER

NOW, this 7th day of December, 1994, following the entry of written Briefs and oral Argument,

IT IS ORDERED that the Plaintiffs' Motion for New Trial is denied.[1]

BY THE COURT:

Robert K. Young, Judge

---

[1]In this medical malpractice case, the Plaintiffs put the Defendant/Doctor through a jury trial on the basis that the doctor misdiagnosed the injuries of the Plaintiff, Mario F. Moses, due to his failure to personally read certain X-rays. Those X-rays were taken at a hospital and were interpreted

CONTINUATION OF FOOTNOTE

---

by a licensed radiologist, upon whose report Dr. Dickson relied. The trial was essentially a "battle of the experts".

The Plaintiffs first ask for a new trial because the Court refused to direct a verdict in their favor following the close of the testimony. The Plaintiffs argue that because Dr. Dickson admitted that he relied on the interpretation of a radiologist regarding the lack of a fracture being shown on the X-ray, and because Dr. Dickson conceded that radiologists do make mistakes, Dr. Dickson was therefore negligent per se. That was also the opinion of the Plaintiffs' expert, Dr. Dunn. However, both of the Defendants' experts testified that they often rely upon a radiologist's report without examining each X-ray personally, and that it was their opinion that such a procedure constituted the standard of care for orthopedic surgeons. Under the above facts, the Court could not determine that Dr. Dickson had committed negligence per se, and properly placed that issue before the jury.

The Plaintiffs further contend that this Court committed a prejudicial error against them by not instructing the jury as to whether or not it was to apply a "local" standard of care or a "national" standard of care. The Court did not use either term in its charge, but simply instructed the jury that "if [the Defendant] falls below that ordinary, prudent, reasonable care standard of those in his profession at the time he does it, that's negligence." (N.T., Vol. I, pp. 346, 347). The concept of local vs. national standard was first raised by the Plaintiffs after the Court's jury charge. That issue was never a part of the Trial. No expert discussed such different standards. Throughout the trial the key dispute among the experts was simply whether or not an orthopedic surgeon complied with his professional standard of care when he relied upon the interpretation of an X-ray by a radiologist, rather than examining each X-ray himself.

The last reason advanced as the basis for a new Trial, is that the Court erred in instructing the jury to disregard

-2-

144

CONTINUATION OF FOOTNOTE

———————————

the expert report of Dr. Mark Cerciello. The Plaintiffs argue that because the defense brought out the fact that the defense experts had, among other documents, reviewed an expert report of Dr. Cerciello, and disagreed with its conclusions, that Dr. Cerciello's report then became admissible and should have been shown to the jury.

Dr. Cerciello was an expert listed as a witness in the Plaintiffs' pre-trial memorandum. His expert report was, as is customary, exchanged with the Defendant. The Defendant sent it to his own experts who "reviewed" it. Dr. DiSalvo did not testify that he relied on any part of Dr. Cerciello's expert report. He stated that he "had" the report, which was supplied to him along with many documents. On cross examination, Plaintiffs' Counsel brought up Dr. Cerciello's report, and even read a small part of it to Dr. DiSalvo, to which Dr. DiSalvo merely replied, "That's what he said." (N.T. pp. 96, 99, 115, 116 and 122).

The Defendants' other orthopedic expert, Dr. Ward, was asked on cross examination if he saw Dr. Cerciello's expert report. Dr. Ward stated that he "didn't recall it." When the report was thereafter located among his papers, he refuted its conclusions. That was the opposite of reliance. (N.T. pp. 278, 279 and 290).

Dr. Cerciello was never called as a witness by the Plaintiff, and the Defendant therefore had no opportunity to cross examine either the doctor or his report. Accordingly, when the jury asked to see the "deposition" of Dr. Cerciello, the Court noted that (a) no deposition of him was ever taken, and therefore the Court could not comply with that request, and (b) because Dr. Cerciello never testified, nor was his expert report "in evidence", the jury should therefore not concern itself with anything Dr. Cerciello may have said or written. Although indeed harmful to the Plaintiffs' case, the ruling was correct. The mere reference by an expert to another expert's report does not make that report admissible. Neither of the Defendants' experts <u>relied</u> upon Dr. Cerciello's report. In that situation, the qualifications of the expert and the quality of his report must be put to the jury only after the opposing side has had a chance to cross examine.

-3-

# JURY TRIALS

My Great-Grandchildren probably visualize me sitting up on a high bench overseeing an important jury trial. The fact is that I only held about one jury trial a month—ten or twelve a year. The courtroom was used extensively, but the great volume of work consisted of days of Support Court, Guilty Pleas, Hearings of all sorts, legal Arguments, juvenile cases, settlement conferences, a solid week of Orphans' Court (where a jury is not used, but which requires hearings and arguments about decedents' estates, trusts, and adoptions) and lots and lots of Orders and Opinions to write. One of the factors causing fewer jury trials was the psychological effect upon the disputing parties when they suddenly saw the jury panel and knew that trial was imminent. Many cases settled just then.

It may not sound very dignified, but a jury trial was in fact a "production." Not exactly a play, but there was an oversized room, a stage, the telling of a story in sort of a Socratic manner by asking lots of questions, and an ending. The participants had defined roles, and knew when to speak or remain silent. There was normally an audience, although they were not permitted to cheer or boo. The main characters often turned out to be the lawyers. There was drama, heightened by the fact that everyone was aware that at least one of the cast was going to feel pain, while others might leave satisfied, or not. There were going to be consequences.

Because of the back-load of work and the need to move cases through the system (the reason our County was approved for a sixth judge), I know that I became a bit testy when the attorneys, clerks, and witnesses were not on time. It was not just my time that was important, but when court was in session, those assembled included myself, a court reporter, sheriff, clerk of one of the Divisions, Court Crier, and whoever was on the other side of the case being heard.

And there was always office work to do.

Whether I was trying a jury case, a support matter, a custody dispute, a name change or any other legal issue, I tried to remember that although I might have handled the same or a similar situation many times, the parties in front of me were probably anxious, sort of like the medical pre-operation anxiety that we all suffer. They needed to know that the judge was not in a bad mood. So, I really tried to be attentive and pleasant.

If, Great-Grandchildren, you are called for jury service, rearrange your schedule and report for duty. Someday you may need a jury to decide a case in which you are involved. I would often talk to jurors after their service. I thanked them and asked them for suggestions and general comments about their experiences as jurors. Almost all jurors, after participating, said that they found the job important and interesting. You will be treated with dignity, probably learn some law, and come to better understand the judicial system's continuing effort to provide a fair way of resolving human legal problems.

As late as the 1950's, our County created a pool of jurors by having the "Ward Leaders" of each political party submit names of those who agreed to serve in advance to a small Board of Jury Commissioners. Those volunteers were chosen by means of a "Jury Wheel." We ended up with panels of jurors who were mostly retired; often hard of hearing; fiscally conservative; and happy for the very small fee they received – quite often serving a few times a year. In civil cases, the amount of the verdicts was exceptionally small, to the point that the lawyers would try to have their cases tried in Philadelphia, where more liberal juries prevailed. We then had only four trial judges, and many fewer cases that needed a jury.

The system of selecting jurors has been changed in several ways. The age of the computer arrived, which made possible a random selection from a large list of County residents who had voted in the last election. A brilliant solution that did not work as planned. Once the word was out, a substantial number of voters (mostly the younger citizens) elected not to vote. The problem of choosing a representative group of peers to act as jurors was solved, at least to my satisfaction, by now picking prospective jurors from a list from the usual sources plus names provided by the Commonwealth's Department of Transportation of those residing in our County who hold valid driver's licenses. The people might give up voting, but never their license to drive! (Incidentally, for the curious, during 2015, out of 38,460 Jury Summons mailed by Lehigh County, 3,761 jurors were sent to the courtroom for jury selection, and of those only 983 were utilized as jurors, or, 2.5% of all those who received a summons.)

Jurors came up with a host of reasons why they ought to be excused. It was my practice to give them not a Hearing, but a conversation about their particular hardship. In most cases, they would eventually explain that "I would like to, but…" That gave me the opening to POSTPONE their service until the next more convenient group of summons was to be mailed. Not excuse them. That postponement information was given to the Jury Selection Administrator, who made a notation for the future.

Most of the requests for excuses were reasonable. If someone in the family was ill, or if the candidate had already paid for a vacation, I did not hesitate to grant a postponement. Some applicants had medical problems, such as very poor hearing, or the need to use a bathroom quickly and often. These I did excuse. Very occasionally I was not satisfied with one of my "conversations" with a prospective juror. I can remember one time when a fairly irate gentleman told me that his employer was going to dock him some pay if he lost time as a juror. I immediately telephoned the employer, who said that no such threat had been made. I kept the irate gentleman in the panel. One man who was to be selected in a criminal case, told me that he just refused to serve, because "all these criminals are guilty." I had the sheriff escort him to the jury selection room, where he was to wait until four o'clock before being excused.

Jury trials sometimes pose a disadvantage for criminal defendants. One reason for the high percentage of guilty pleas is that the sentencing judge is normally given a fairly brief report by the District Attorney regarding the events that created one or more crimes. The District Attorney will normally drop some of the charges. If the case is to be heard by a jury it will also be simultaneously heard by the judge. That judge will be doing the sentencing, and will learn a great deal more about all of the defendant's criminal behavior. It has been my experience that a defendant who is convicted by a jury receives a meaningful increase in his sentencing over a defendant who pleads guilty for the same offences. There should be no penalty for using a jury, but I believe that was the realistic fact when I was on the bench. However, I did not think that I should advise a Defendant about the possible adverse effects of a jury trial at the time of sentencing. That might well look as though I was trying to persuade him or her to enter a guilty plea.

# LAWSUITS AGAINST PROFESSIONALS: THE HALPERIN CASE

Lawsuits against professionals not only include doctors, as in the preceding Moses case, but also accountants, engineers, teachers, police, lawyers and probably every other type of service giver.

I did not handle any cases of malpractice against attorneys, although I am aware that they occur. All good lawyers carry errors and omissions insurance coverage. There are special provisions regarding the protection of a lawyer's trust accounts, and all practicing attorneys must attend substantial hours of continuing legal education each year.

The Halperin Complaint against his C.P.A., pled two separate causes of action. One sounded in fraud, the other alleged a breach of a confidential relationship. The Defendant brought a Motion for Summary Judgment, asking me to hold that both of those actions were defective. I denied that request as to the fraud count, so that the case could proceed to Discovery and eventual trial. I granted the Summary Motion as to the separate claim of the breach of a confidential relationship for the reasons set forth in my April Opinion and January Order with footnote. That may sound technical, but over the years, the law has established specific factual criteria that must be met in order to successfully sue someone for a recognized "Cause of Action."

CIVIL ACTION - LAW

EDWARD HALPERIN and
MARION HALPERIN,                    )
                                    )
                                    )
        Plaintiffs                  )
                                    )
                                    )
        vs.                         )    No. 89-C-2711
                                    )
        J.                          )
                                    )
                                    )
        Defendant                   )

## ORDER

NOW, this 4ᵗʰ day of January, 1992, upon consideration of written Briefs and oral Argument of counsel, and consistent with the accompanying footnote,

IT IS ORDERED that Defendant's Motion for Summary Judgment is Granted in part and Denied in part.[1]

BY THE COURT:

Robert K. Young, Judge

---

[1] The Defendant,      J      , is a Certified Public Accountant. He was employed by the Plaintiffs, Edward and Marion Halperin (Halperins), to perform accounting services and give financial advice. This relationship existed from 1975 until 1984. During this period, the Halperins, on

## CONTINUATION OF FOOTNOTE

---

J.        's recommendations, invested in four tax shelters.

Following an IRS investigation, three of the four tax shelters were found to be improper deductions. The Halperins were ordered to pay back taxes, interest and penalties. During the IRS investigation, the Halperins sought and received J.      's advice and services.

After the IRS investigation was concluded, the Halperins learned that the tax shelters were recommended to J.      by a Mr. Poris (Poris). Poris was a business associate and a friend of J.      's. The Halperins allege that J. received from Poris a commission based upon the monies he obtained on the sales of the tax shelters, and that at no time during their relationship did J.      disclose this fact to them. The three tax shelters are presently economic failures, which have resulted in the Halperins losing their investments. The Halperins are pursuing claims of common law fraud and breach of confidential relations against J.      . J.      is presently seeking summary judgment against both claims.

The standard of review for a summary judgment motion is not easy for a movant to overcome. It has been consistently stated that:

> ...summary judgment may be granted when
> the moving party is entitled to judgment
> as a matter of law and when there is no
> genuine issue of material fact. Such
> judgment should be granted only where
> the right is clear and free from doubt.
> In making this determination, the Trial
> Court must examine the record in the
> light most favorable to the non-moving
> party. (citation omitted).

Mullen v. Borough of Parkesburg, ____ Pa. Cmwlth. ____, ____, 572 A.2d 859, 860-61 (1990). This is the burden that J.      must meet before his motion for summary judgment can be granted.

-2-

CONTINUATION OF FOOTNOTE

---

The Depositions of Edward F. Halperin, Marion Halperin, and
J        were taken.  The following is testimony from
those depositions: J        told me we should investigate tax
shelters (E. Halperin, N.T. p. 20); the Halperins became
interested in the tax shelters for economic reasons as well
as saving money on taxes (E. Halperin, N.T. p. 24); J
was to investigate potential tax shelters for the Halperins
(E. Halperin, N.T. p. 22-24); J        received information
regarding other tax shelters but only pursued those tax
shelters recommended by Poris (J        , N.T. pp 20-21, 30);
J        never mentioned Poris' name or his relationship with
him when they invested in the tax shelters (E. Halperin,
N.T. pp. 32-33, 96-100); the Halperins had complete faith in
J        (E. Halperin, N.T. pp. 34-35); we invested in Lynn
Properties without reading the circular (E. Halperin, N.T.
p. 33); the Halperins didn't invest in two shelters offered
by another party on J        's assurance they were no good (E.
Halperin, N.T. pp. 44-50, 53-57).  If I had known about
J        's dealings with Poris it would have been like waving
a red flag in front of my eyes and I would have realized
that I can't rely on J        for everything he says.  I would
have started looking at other things and not given him carte
blanche (N.T. pp. 99-100).

The elements of common law fraud are well known.  This
Court finds that in considering the above facts a cause of
action in common law fraud could be found to exist by a
jury.  The omission of J        in failing to tell of his
involvement with Poris is a material misrepresentation.  The
objectivity of Defendant in recommending tax shelters to the
Halperins is questionable and had the Halperins known of
J        s involvement with Poris they may have appraised the
recommended tax shelters in a different light.

If the above facts are true, it is also clear that J
had knowledge of the omission but chose not to divulge it.
The tax shelter recommendations were meant to induce
Plaintiffs to invest, which put money into J        .'s pockets.
The relationship that existed between them was such that a
jury could find that the Halperins not only relied upon
J        but trusted him, thus forming a confidential

-3-

CONTINUATION OF FOOTNOTE

---

relationship.

There is no precise definition for what constitutes a confidential relationship. It is deemed to exist when the relative positions of the parties are such that one has the power or means to take advantage or exercise undue influence over the other. See Matter of Estate of Evasew, ___ Pa. ___, 584 A.2d 910 (1990). "When the relationship between persons is one of trust and confidence, the party to whom the trust and confidence are reposed must act with scrupulous fairness and good faith in his dealings with the other and refrain from using his position to the other's detriment and his own advantage. Id. quoting, Young v. Kaye, 443 Pa. 335, 279 A.2d 759 (1971) (emphasis added).

A confidential relationship can generally exist between agent and principle. While such a relationship is not automatically confidential as a matter of a law, it can be found to exist by the factfinder. See Drob v. Jaffe, 351 Pa. 297, 41 A.2d 407 (1945). A finding that a breach of a confidential relationship did occur constitutes constructive or implied fraud. Evasew at ___, 584 A.2d at 912 (1990).

There is thus a genuine issue of material fact as to whether a confidential relationship existed between J and the Halperins. The method in which the Halperins accepted J 's financial advice and believed him to be their "financial advisor" in dealing with other members of the financial communities can be viewed as a relationship founded on trust and confidence to which fiduciary duties are attached.

However, there is no case law suggesting that a breach of a confidential relationship constitutes a separate cause of action independent of fraud. The finding of such a relationship can only aid in establishing fraud. We therefore grant Summary Judgment as to Count II.

-4-

# AND NEXT, A TEACHER'S TERMINATION:

IN THE COURT OF COMMON PLEAS OF LEHIGH COUNTY, PENNSYLVANIA

CIVIL DIVISION - LAW

| | |
|---|---|
| SCHOOL DISTRICT OF THE<br>CITY OF ALLENTOWN,<br><br>　　　　Petitioner<br><br>　　　　vs.<br><br>ALLENTOWN EDUCATION<br>ASSOCIATION and<br>MICHAEL C.<br><br>　　　　Respondents | No. 89-C-218 |

\* \* \* \* \*

APPEARANCES:

　　　EDWARD H. FEEGE, ESQUIRE,
　　　And with him, DUANE, MORRIS & HECKSCHER,
　　　　On behalf of the School District of the
　　　　City of Allentown, Petitioner.

　　　A. MARTIN HERRING, ESQUIRE,
　　　And with him, A. MARTIN HERRING & ASSOCIATES,
　　　　On behalf of the Allentown Education
　　　　Association and Michael C.　　　Respondents.

\* \* \* \* \*

### OPINION

ROBERT K. YOUNG, Judge.

On June 21, 1989 this Court entered an Order which in essence sustained the decision of the Board of Directors of the School District of the City of Allentown in terminating the teaching contract of Mr. Michael C. ____ A footnote was appended to that Order, in which the facts, law and reasoning of the Court were set forth.    That footnote is incorporated by this reference into this Opinion.

Pursuant to Rule 1925(b) the Court asked for a concise statement of the reasons for the appeal so that it might address the Appellant's concerns in this Opinion.    In answer, the Court received a statement which contains the conclusions that:    (1) the Trial Court erred in determining that the Arbitrator's award was not rationally derived from the collective bargaining agreement; (2) the Court failed to examine the language of that agreement; (3) the Court failed to recognize the issue of the case; and (4) the Court applied the wrong law.

It is difficult to meaningfully address the above complaints.    The Trial Court has, however, read each of the appellate cases cited in paragraph 6 of the Respondent's Answer to the Court's Rule 1925(b) Order.  Many of the cases deal with procedural matters (injunctive relief, standard of review, effect of "past practices", etc.).    Some of the cases deal with tenure, while others focus on the finality

-2-

of the Arbitrator's decision with regard to economic issues. None of the holdings relate to the discipline of a teacher, which under the rationale of Liquor Control Bd. v. Independent State Stores Union, ___ Pa. ___, 553 A.2d 948 (1989) is the unalienable duty of the governmental agency. Only the question of whether there was "just cause" for discipline should be decided by the Arbitrator.

In Community College of Beaver County v. Community College of Beaver County, the Society of Faculty (PSEA/NEA), 473 Pa. 576, 375 A.2d 1267 (1977), which held that the Arbitrator was correct in deciding that under the applicable labor agreement teachers who had been laid off for economic reasons were to be given preference when re-hirings were made, Justice Pomeroy discusses the fact-finding obligations of the Arbitrator as opposed to the law-finding functions of the Court. He distinguishes those separate functions, and of course reserves matters of law to the judiciary.

In the case now on appeal, the Trial Court has not found any error with the Arbitrator's factual decision that just cause did exist upon which the School Board was justified in disciplining **[ Michael C. ]** That was the arbitratable issue at hand. However, it is the opinion of this Lower Court Judge, based upon the rulings of the

Appellate Courts of this Commonwealth in analagous situations, that the Arbitrator did not have the legal authority to reset the penalty which was imposed by the School Board.  There are certain duties which attach to every elected official.  No matter what the collective bargaining agreement specified, it is the School Board which must by law cast its vote in open sessions.  It must not delegate its responsibility to set the calendar; to establish the curriculum; to hire qualified administrators, teaching professionals, solicitors, architects, maintenance personnel, etc.; to set the tax millage; to approve textbooks; and a host of other duties referred to in Section 5 of The Public School Code (24 P.S. 5-501 et. seq.).  Specifically, "appointing or dismissing ... teachers," must be accomplished by a majority of all of the Directors (not merely of a quorum), the vote of each member to be separately recorded.  24 P.S. §5-508.  Those same requirements are repeated in §5-508 (item 9) as follows: "Dismissing a teacher after a hearing."  Thus, an arbitrator does not have the legal power to consider the entire range of possible sanctions.  How then can he sit in judgment as to the proper recourse for reprimand -- and how can he overrule a board decision over which he has no legal jurisdiction?   The legislature has wisely required that it is the School Board which must hire and, if necessary, fire, upon just cause.

Discipline may be less severe than dismissal, just as probation is less onerous than jail. But just as trial courts cannot by law delegate their sentencing duties, not even to another judge, so, too, school boards should be held accountable for the punishment or praise of those whom they have engaged to carry out the public service of educating our citizens.

BY THE COURT:

Robert K. Young, Judge

Dated:   August 31, 1989

The review of the dismissal of an Allentown Police officer follows.

IN THE COURT OF COMMON PLEAS OF LEHIGH COUNTY, PENNSYLVANIA

CIVIL ACTION - LAW

|  |  |  |
|---|---|---|
| O' | ) | |
| Plaintiff | ) | |
| vs. | ) | No. 90-C-0254 |
| CITY OF ALLENTOWN, | ) | |
| Defendant | ) | |

ORDER

NOW, this 7ᵗʰ day of September, 1994, following an examination of the entire record and exhibits, the entry of written Briefs and oral Argument,

IT IS ORDERED that the action of Allentown City Council in dismissing O' as a police officer on the charge of Conduct Unbecoming an Officer, is affirmed.[1]

BY THE COURT:

*Robert K. Young*

Robert K. Young, Judge

---

[1] O' was employed as a police officer by the City of Allentown, Pennsylvania, for more

CONTINUATION OF FOOTNOTE

---

than eighteen (18) years. During that period, he received many letters of commendation for specific acts of courtesy and bravery, but also received four suspensions. He has been dismissed from the force by action of the City's Council, upon recommendation of the Mayor and Chief of Police, following a series of Hearings.

Counsel for the City and O'_____ have stipulated that although 53 P.S. §39408 specifies that a de novo Hearing is to be held by the Court of Common Pleas in these matters, the Court is to base its decision as to whether or not O'_____ was properly dismissed upon the Record produced during City Council's proceedings. No additional testimony having been taken or offered, it is the opinion of the Court that the principles of Hart v. City of Coatesville, 22 Chest. 325 (1974) and City of New Kensington v. Swierczewski, 50 Mun. 242, 41 West. 27, 1959, are to be applied. That is, the Court must not substitute its judgment for that of City Council if the evidence supports the discretion exercised by that body, and the Court is to consider prior acts and suspensions in determining whether or not Council may have abused its discretion in imposing a dismissal of the officer.

The Mayor and Chief of Police suspended O'_____ until the matter could be heard by City Council. The charges were that he engaged in conduct unbecoming a police officer. That general accusation consists of "any conduct which adversely affects the morale or efficiency of the bureau to which [the officer] is assigned...[and] is also any conduct which has a tendency to destroy public respect for municipal employees and confidence in the operation of municipal services." Zeber Appeal, 398 Pa. 35, 43, 156 A.2d 821, 825 (1959). The burden of proof by a preponderance of the credible evidence is upon the City.

The undisputed facts are that O'_____ while off duty in plain clothes, entered a jail cell at City Hall in which a man was being held, shackled by his leg to a bench. O'_____ approached the man "nose to nose", and engaged in a physical altercation with the man resulting in the tearing

-2-

CONTINUATION OF FOOTNOTE

———————————————

out of a substantial amount of the man's hair.   O'
was evicted from the cell by other on-duty officers, but
several minutes later re-entered the cell, after which he
was again ordered to leave.

Those simple facts were witnessed by at least two officers,
and were admitted as being true by          .   Other direct
evidence, if believed by City Council, established that
O'          hit the victim with either a blackjack or
flashlight, and that O'          entered the cell on both
occasions without just cause.   The first time O'
entered, the victim was subdued, causing no difficulty, and
the second time O'          testified that he was just curious
because of a "commotion" that was occurring.

   O'          justifies his conduct or, in the alternative,
seeks a reduction of his punishment, on the basis that the
victim had on an earlier occasion appeared at O'
wife's home, asking for and threatening to "get" O'
O'          had reported that harassment to his superiors, but
felt that they were not doing enough to stop the victim's
conduct.

The above synopsis is admittedly brief, but it contains the
central facts.   In his closing argument, O'          counsel
correctly states, "Now he's made a mistake.   And it's a big
one.   It's not something that should by any stretch of the
imagination go unpunished."   It is clear that engaging in a
fight with a shackled prisoner is wrong, and that it
logically brings the police department into disrespect by
the community.   That being the case, the morale of the
department is naturally adversely affected.   One of the
officers reported that she was "shocked" by what happened.
It is, therefore, concluded that City Council did have
substantial credible evidence to support its finding that
O'          did engage in conduct unbecoming an officer.

In view of the fact that O'          had already been
suspended on four prior occasions, and the seriousness of
this latest incident, the Court cannot hold that City
Council abused its discretion in imposing the sanction of

-3-

160

CONTINUATION OF FOOTNOTE

———————————

dismissal. A policeman's job is known to be both important and difficult. O'_____ acknowledged that he was under a great deal of stress due to family problems and police work. He candidly admitted that he had tried to obtain psychological counseling, but that he was unable to find the time, and further stated that he was "not qualified to say" whether he was fit to return to police work, although he thought he was.

The loss of this position is surely a hard blow to Mr. O'_____ As noted, he gave satisfactory service to the community for over 18 years. The Court is not prepared to hold, however, that City Council abused its discretion in this case. Sometimes one mistake is so serious that it warrants strong punishment. O'_____ was reportedly found not guilty of any criminal charges arising out of this incident. That ruling is not determinative as to these proceedings, where the burden of proof is considerably less, and the parties to the action different.

Furthermore, the fact that City Council held its Hearing before those criminal charges were tried is also not a controlling issue. O'_____ testified voluntarily at the City Council Hearing, and did not invoke his Fifth Amendment rights. City Council had a legitimate concern that any prolonged delay in making its decision would work a great harm on the morale of the police force and the confidence in that organization by the public. O'_____ acted rashly, for personal reasons, and struck a shackled prisoner. His actions were well explained and are understood, but the Court cannot fault City Council for its reaction in ordering his dismissal.

# THE WHISTLEBLOWER CASE

In 1992, I made a difficult decision regarding the dismissal of an employee. Equity and Justice were on his side, but the law was against him. I would not have minded being reversed by the Superior Court, but it sustained my ruling to deny the Plaintiff a new trial.

The above comment brings to mind a policy I used in writing footnotes and opinions. Before I started to express the reasons for my conclusion, I focused on whom the prime persons were that most needed to know what I had decided. In the Krajsa whistleblower case, I was talking to the Superior Court Judges. In N. E. S., where the parents had asked the Court to allow the withdrawal of life-support from their daughter, my words were directed to them. Some opinions were aimed at the lawyers, others at various public agencies. A few, such as the Hospital Cases regarding sufficient charitable care, and the Adjudications regarding the fiduciary duties of executors and trustees, were written for a much wider audience.

IN THE COURT OF COMMON PLEAS OF LEHIGH COUNTY, PENNSYLVANIA
CIVIL DIVISION - LAW

MICHAEL J. KRAJSA,            )
                             )
          Plaintiff           )
                             )
     vs.                      )    No. 87-C-1361
                             )
KEYPUNCH, INC., DIANE         )
COLFER, ROBERT B. COLFER,     )
                             )
          Defendants          )

\* \* \* \* \*

APPEARANCES:

      DONALD E. WIEAND, JR., ESQUIRE,
      And with him, WEAVER, MOSEBACH,
      PIOSA, HIXSON & MARLES,
        On behalf of the Plaintiff.

      MARK MALKAMES, ESQUIRE,
      And with him, MALKAMES LAW OFFICES,
        On behalf of the Defendants.

\* \* \* \* \*

## OPINION

The Plaintiff was an "at-will" employee of the Defendants. He seeks damages for a wrongful discharge, alleging that he was fired because he told the Commonwealth of Pennsylvania that the Defendants were violating their contracts with that government, by billing for work not actually performed.  The case was called for trial on January 6, 1992.  That morning the Defendant (Colfer) presented a Motion for Summary Judgment and Exclusion of Evidence.  The Court ruled that the motion was untimely and proceeded with the trial.

The opening arguments were presented, and the Plaintiff (Krajsa) was called as the first witness.  Krajsa was on the verge of offering evidence regarding his wrongful discharge when Colfer objected.  The jury was recessed, and the Court, after argument from both sides and a careful review of the law, reluctantly sustained Colfer's objections, ruling that any testimony regarding the claim for wrongful discharge was irrelevant for the reasons discussed below.

The trial continued solely on Krajsa's claim for unpaid commissions.  After four days of trial, the jury deliberated and found that a contract for commissions existed between the parties, but that Krajsa was not entitled to them.  Krajsa then filed Post Trial Motions which are the subject of this Opinion.

Krajsa argues that:  the Court improperly granted an involuntary non-suit before he had ended his case in

-2-

chief. Further, he believes that the preclusion of the wrongful discharge claim was in error, and that he should have been permitted to impeach the credibility of Robert Colfer by the disallowed testimony.

This Court did not grant an involuntary non-suit. The exclusion of the Plaintiff's testimony concerning the bad acts of Defendant Colfer was an evidentiary ruling. Under the facts of the case no cause of action existed, and any evidence presented on that issue was irrelevant.

Generally, there is no cause of action against an employer for termination of an at-will employment relationship. Geary v. United States Steel Corp., 456 Pa. 171, 319 A.2d 174 (1974). "Exceptions to this rule have been recognized in only the most limited of circumstances, where discharges of at-will employees would threaten clear mandates of public policy." Clay v. Advanced Computer Applications, Inc., 522 Pa. 86, 559 A.2d 917 (1989), citing Reuther v. Fowler & Williams, Inc., 255 Pa. Super. 28, 386 A.2d 119 (1978). The termination must violate significant and recognized public policies which strike at the heart of a citizen's social right, duties and responsibilities. Yetter v. Ward Trucking Corp., ___ Pa. Super. ___, 585 A.2d

-3-

1022, 1026 (1991).

> The sources of public policy [which may limit the employer's right of discharge] include legislation; administrative rules, regulation, or decision; and judicial decision. In certain instances, a professional code of ethics may contain an expression of public policy.... Absent legislation, the judiciary must define the cause of action in case-by-case determinations.

Id. citing Pierce v. Ortho Pharmaceutical Corp., 84 N.J. 58, 72, 417 A.2d 505, 512 (1980).

In the few cases where the Appellate Courts have upheld a claim for the wrongful discharge of an at-will employee, the decision has been supported by a statute evidencing a clear legislative public policy. See, Field v. Philadelphia Electric Co., 388 Pa. Super. 400, 565 A.2d 1170 (1989); Hunter v Port. Auth. of Allegheny County, 277 Pa. Super. 4, 419 A.2d 631 (1980); Reuther, supra.

Krajsa argues that a strong public policy exists to report to the appropriate authorities fraudulent billing practices and fraudulent non-performance of governmental contracts. Krajsa punctuates this by arguing that the Whistle-Blower statute, formulated to prevent such waste and fraud, is applicable. This Court agrees that individuals

-4-

who contract with the government and who then perpetrate fraud and waste in fulfilling their services should be reported. Such activities do "strike at the heart of a citizen's social right, duty, and responsibility." While the alleged acts of Colfer are reprehensible, there is no specific statute or judicially recognized public policy condemning it. The Whistle-Blower statute defines employee as:

> "Employee: A person who performs a service for wages or other remuneration under a contract of hire, written or oral, express or implied, for a public body."

43 P.S. Section 1422.

Krajsa was not employed by a public body but by a private citizen performing a public contract. While it may be viewed that this is a distinction without a difference, it is not this Court's prerogative to legislate. If the legislature intended to afford the same protection to persons working for employers who have government contracts, it would have specifically enumerated such language. All that would have been needed was the addition of the words "for a public or private body." It is sometimes difficult

-5-

to ascertain the intent of the Legislative Branch, but it may well have been concerned with opening up a flood of litigation between the millions of employers and their employees in the private sector.

A Trial Court should not distort a statute to afford relief not specifically included. It was Colfer's prerogative to terminate Krajsa without justification at any time. Darlington v. General Electric, 350 Pa. Super. 183, 504 A.2d 306 (1986).

\* \* \* \* \*

Krajsa in the alternative argues that the information he gathered to prove his alleged claims of fraud and waste should have been allowed to impeach Colfer.

It is well established that evidence of specific bad acts may not be introduced in a civil case to impeach a witness. Butler v. Flo-Ron Vending Co., 383 Pa. Superior 633, 557 A.2d 730 (1989), citing Berliner v. Schoerberg, 117 Pa. Super. 254, 178 A.2d 330 (1935). The Court may not

-6-

properly allow questions to be put to a witness concerning his guilt of some alleged crime for which he was never convicted. Id.

If any party was prejudiced, it was the Defendant, because the jury was told by Plaintiff's Counsel in the openings about the fraud and waste Colfer perpetrated on the government.

The Post-Trial Motion of the Plaintiff is Denied.

BY THE COURT:

Robert K. Young, Judge

Dated: June 10 , 1992.

The Superior Court noted that its research had discovered that only three Pennsylvania courts have held that a claim for unlawful discharge by a private employer was proper: (1) where the discharge was based on the duty to report nuclear safety violations under federal law, (2) the denial of employment to a person on the basis of a prior conviction for which he had been pardoned, and (3) where a person was discharged when required to appear for jury duty. Thus, government employees are protected from being fired for reporting fraud, but not employees of a private company, even if a defense contractor.

# SOVEREIGN IMMUNITY

Further, our State, and all of the local municipalities and their agencies, are protected by statutes granting them immunity if their employees negligently cause damage to others in a variety of situations. An example of how that works is the following Bollinger case, dealing with an ancient British doctrine adopted by Pennsylvania and set forth in our "Sovereign Immunity Act." We gave up Sovereigns in 1776. The appropriate name for the defense against liability is Governmental Immunity.

IN THE COURT OF COMMON PLEAS OF LEHIGH COUNTY, PENNSYLVANIA

CIVIL ACTION - LAW

KELLIE BOLLINGER, a minor )
by ELSIE CARRAGHAN, her )
guardian, and ELSIE )
CARRAGHAN, )
)
    Plaintiffs )
)
    vs. ) No. 86-C-1115
)
THEODORE OBRECHT, EAST PENN )
SCHOOL DISTRICT and LEHIGH )
COUNTY VOCATIONAL TECHNICAL )
SCHOOL, )
)
    Defendants )

\* \* \* \* \*

APPEARANCES:

    MALCOLM J. GROSS, ESQUIRE,
    And with him, GROSS, McGINLEY, LaBARRE & EATON,
      On behalf of the Plaintiffs.

    ROBERT J. HANNA, JR., ESQUIRE,
    And with him, MARSHALL, DENNEHEY, WARNER,
    COLEMAN AND GOGGIN,
      On behalf of the Defendants.

\* \* \* \* \*

OPINION

ROBERT K. YOUNG, Judge.

    Rule 1035 permits entry of Summary Judgment where

there are no genuine issues as to material fact and when a party has demonstrated that he or she is entitled to such judgment as a matter of law. Pa. R.C.P. 1035(b); <u>Thorsen v. Iron and Glass Bank</u>, 328 Pa. Super. 135 476 A.2d 928 (1984). In <u>Kotwasinski v. Rasner</u>, 436 Pa. 32, 258 A.2d 865 (1969), the Supreme Court ruled that Summary Judgment is to be granted only in the "clearest of cases". As noted by the Superior Court in <u>Ritmanich v. Jonnel Enterprises, Inc.</u>, 219 Pa. Super. 198, 203, 280 A.2d 570 (1971), "... we are to accept as true all well-pleaded facts in the non-moving parties' pleadings, as well as the admissions on file, giving them the benefit of all reasonable inferences to be drawn therefrom; and in passing upon a motion for Summary Judgment, it is no part of our function to decide issues of fact but solely to determine whether there is an issue of fact to be tried and all doubts as to the existence of a genuine issue as to a material fact must be resolved against the party moving for Summary Judgment".

Kellie Bollinger, the Plaintiff (hereinafter referred to as Miss Bollinger), was fifteen (15) years old on January 18, 1985, when it is alleged that she was operating a printing press on the premises of the Defendant Lehigh County Vocational-Technical School (hereinafter

-2-

172

designated as the School) under the supervision of her teacher, the Defendant Theodore Obrecht (hereinafter designated as Obrecht). Two of her fingers became caught in the rollers or cylinders of a printing press, injuring her index finger and the long finger of her right hand causing fractures of the distal phalanges. The press is known as a Chief 15, and was donated to the School several years before the accident. Miss Bollinger alleges that she received one-on-one instruction from Obrecht regarding the correct use of the press, and that on the day of the accident she attempted to instruct a fellow student on its proper operation. While she was in the process of instructing her classmate, someone walked into the room and momentarily distracted her. It was at this time that she was injured.

Miss Bollinger and her mother, Elsie Carraghan, instituted suit against the School and Obrecht (as well as the "home" School District of East Penn, which has by Stipulation been dismissed from the case). It is alleged inter alia, that both the School and Obrecht failed to provide guards and/or other safety devices on the printing press to prevent injury to the Plaintiff; failed to otherwise enclose the printing press cylinders; failed to properly instruct and supervise Miss Bollinger in the use

-3-

and maintenance of the press; and failed to warn her of the danger involved in its use and maintenance.

At his Deposition, Defendant Obrecht testified that the printing press in question is not attached to the floor in any manner, nor was it ever attached to the floor. He characterized the press as a portable piece of equipment. Obrecht further explained that a guard did not come with the press but that one was fabricated at his direction to prevent someone's fingers from slipping into the machine. The record indicates that the guard in question was not in place at the time Obrecht instructed Plaintiff on the operation of the press, nor was it in place at the time that she used the press. He opined that there was a danger involved in using the press without the guard being present.

The School and Obrecht allege that Miss Bollinger's claim is barred in that it does not fall under the real property exception to the general Sovereign immunity provisions found in 42 Pa. C.S.A. Section 8542(b) (or any other exception to immunity) or, alternatively, that her claim for damages is barred by 42 Pa. C.S.A. Section 8553(c) regarding certain types of recognized losses.

The real property exception found in 42 Pa. C.S.A. Section 8542(b)(3) provides the following:

-4-

(b) Acts which may impose liability - the following acts by a local agency or any of its employees may result in the imposition of liability on a local agency:
(3) Real Property - The care, custody or control of real property in the possession of the local agency, except that the local agency shall not be liable for damages on account of any injury sustained by a person intentionally trespassing on real property in the possession of the local agency . . .

The Supreme Court of Pennsylvania in <u>Mascaro v. Youth Study Center</u>, ___ Pa. ___, 523 A.2d 1118, 1123, (1987), explained:

The real estate exception to governmental immunity is a narrow exception and, by its own terms, refers only to injuries arising out of the care, custody or control of the real property in the possession of the political subdivision or its employees. Acts of the local agency or its employees which make the property unsafe for the activities for which it is regularly used, for which it is intended to be used, or for which it may reasonably be foreseen to be used, are acts which make the local agency amenable to suit.

In <u>Mascaro</u>, the Supreme Court held that "the real estate exception can be applied only to those cases where it is alleged that the artificial condition or defect of the land itself causes the injury not merely when it facilitates the injury by the acts of others, whose acts are outside the

-5-

statute's scope of liability". 523 A.2d at 1124 (1987).

The Defendants argue that the printing press in question is a mobile piece of equipment, not affixed or attached to the floor of the classroom in any manner and that therefore Summary Judgment should be granted because "real estate" is not involved. Plaintiff argues that the printing press in question is a fixture, and therefore part of the real estate. In McCloskey v. Abington School District, ___ Pa. Commw. ___, 515 A.2d 642, 645, (1986), the Commonwealth Court stated, "the question of the intent of the parties makes most decisions on whether fixtures are real estate a matter for a fact-finder rather than something that can be decided as a matter of law by the Court". Furthermore, the Court in McCloskey cited an article by George B. Clothier entitled The Law of Fixtures in Pennsylvania, 32 Pa. B.Q. 66 (1960-61) which states in pertinent part:

> The factors which determine whether or not a chattel becomes a "fixture" when annexed to the land include (a) the manner in which it is physically attached or installed, (b) the extent to which it is essential to the permanent use of the building or other improvement, and (c) the intention of the parties who attached or installed it. As to intent, it is not so much what a particular

-6-

party intended his legal rights to be, as it is what intended use of the property was manifested by the conduct of the parties.

The decisional law on what does or does not become a fixture divides real estate generally into two classes - dwellings and industrial establishments. As to both, the intended use of the chattel is the dominant factor; but for reasons which are logical enough when carefully considered the treatment of completely unattached chattels as fixtures is limited to the industrial plant. The value of a dwelling - single or multiple - derives from the common use to which every unfurnished unit can be put; the chattels installed by the occupant are personal to him and to her, and their removal does not substantially diminish the value of the home or its income producing capacity as living accommodations for another family.

A factory or other industrial building, however, while it may be suitable, depending on the machinery with which it is equipped, for any number of different industrial uses, derives its principal value from the particular going concern which it houses. The profits of that business, or the economic function, whatever it may be, of building and contents together, supply the basis for appraising the property, and the security for the mortgage lender. Hence the rule that machinery and equipment, fast or loose, necessary to the business conducted in the building, falls within the category of fixtures. Office furniture and equipment, however, do not become fixtures.

In the case at bar, the Plaintiff has alleged sufficient facts to surpass the Motion for Summary Judgment filed by the Defendants with respect to the real estate exception to governmental immunity.

~7~

In the Bollinger case, I decided that the School District defense that it was immune from suit had not been clearly proven. Whether the printing press was a part of the real estate or not was a question for the jury. The School District appealed. All seven judges of the Commonwealth Court joined in a nine-page Opinion that ended with the words: "Accordingly, we quash the appeal."

The Court decided that it had no jurisdiction because my denial of a Defendant's Motion for Summary Judgment was not an appealable "final" order. The case could go on. I especially enjoyed the Court's use of a word that everyone can understand, "Quash."

A second and shorter Order and footnote represents an effort by one governmental agency, the Pennsylvania Department of Transportation, to keep the Borough of Emmaus as a Defendant in a negligence case so that the borough would need to share in paying for the damages. Did the borough escape?

IN THE COURT OF COMMON PLEAS OF LEHIGH COUNTY, PENNSYLVANIA

CIVIL DIVISION - LAW

RICHARD OLHANOSKI and )
DONNA OLHANOSKI, his wife, )
                        )
        Plaintiffs )
                        )
        vs. )   No. 89-C-176
                        )
COMMONWEALTH OF PENNSYLVANIA, )
DEPARTMENT OF TRANSPORTATION, )
and BOROUGH OF EMMAUS, )
                        )
        Defendants )

## ORDER

NOW, this   $20^{2}$   day of July, 1992, upon consideration of written Briefs of Counsel, and consistent with the accompanying footnote,

IT IS ORDERED that Defendants' Motion for Summary Judgment is Granted.[1]

BY THE COURT:

Robert K. Young / Judge

---

[1]This is the third motion for summary judgment considered by the Court in this case. This time the Borough of Emmaus (Emmaus) is the petitioner. Emmaus contends that although

CONTINUATION OF FOOTNOTE

---

they own the property on which the accident took place, their jurisdiction was relinquished to the Commonwealth of Pennsylvania, Department of Transportation (PennDOT). PennDOT was granted exclusive jurisdiction and control of the property when they were ordered by the Public Utilities Commission to repair the drainage system for the roadway. It was during these repairs that the Plaintiff, an employee of a company hired by PennDOT to do the drainage work, was injured.

PennDOT argues that the focus should not be on jurisdiction but ownership, and that Emmaus is not entitled to governmental immunity because it had actual notice of the dangerous conditions. This actual notice was a result of the involvement of Borough inspectors during this project; their work on a sewer break; and the Borough's payment of 17% of the total cost of the project.

There is no doubt that the Emmaus Public Works Director, Daniel A. Delong (Delong) and the Inspector of Public Works, Paul Beiber (Beiber) were involved with the project in a limited nature. They were the persons in charge of all of the Borough's activity regarding its sewers, water systems, highways and parks. However, this was not a Borough project. Their duties were merely to make sure that the PennDOT project was appropriately done in that it did not affect any of the services provided to the public by Emmaus or that the property Emmaus owned was not damaged, as was the case when PennDOT damaged Emmaus' sewer lines. These were the reasons why Delong and Bieber were at the construction site and why they inspected the work.

There is no evidence that Emmaus took an active role in overseeing the construction. While it is clear their expertise was consulted to avoid other problems, they were not immediately involved nor did they supervise this project. Therefore, no actual notice or inference that they should have known of the dangerous condition exists.

PennDOT was ordered to perform the work; they hired the Plaintiff's employer; they planned and oversaw the work; and

-2-

CONTINUATION OF FOOTNOTE

_____

participated in the decision which sent the Plaintiff into the trench which collapsed. This Court will not allow them to dispense with their duty merely because Emmaus owned the land which PennDOT was required to maintain. This Court firmly stands by its prior decision that Plaintiff's injury took place on a highway under PennDOT's control and jurisdiction.

The last of the Governmental Immunity cases might be repetitive in telling you about the types of legal entanglements on which the trial courts work, but the facts beg exposure. Their recitation by the Commonwealth Court is superior to my footnote.

IN THE COMMONWEALTH COURT OF PENNSYLVANIA

THEODORE          and GLORIA    :
    as Parents and Natural:
Guardians of DAVID ,          :
and THEODORE and GLORIA        :
       Individually,          :
          Appellants           :   No. 2394 C.D. 1994
                               :   Argued: April 3, 1995
       v.                      :
                               :
LEHIGH COUNTY OFFICE OF        :
CHILDREN AND YOUTH SERVICES    :

BEFORE:   HONORABLE JAMES GARDNER COLINS, President Judge
          HONORABLE JOSEPH T. DOYLE, Judge (P.)
          HONORABLE EMIL E. NARICK, Senior Judge

OPINION BY PRESIDENT JUDGE COLINS          FILED: May 18, 1995

Theodore and Gloria          , as Parents and Natural Guardians of David          (David), and Theodore and Gloria Individually (Appellants), appeal from an order of the Court of Common Pleas of Lehigh County (Common Pleas) granting a motion for judgment on the pleadings filed by the Lehigh County Office of Children and Youth Services (CYS).

The record indicates that in 1974, Appellants sought the services of CYS to adopt a child. After what Appellants aver were "extensive consultations," CYS recommended they adopt a young boy named David and provided Appellants with a one-page report stating that David's biological father and mother were both "in good health." Sometime after the adoption, David exhibited serious behavioral problems that, on May 16, 1990, culminated in his setting Appellants' home on fire.

Subsequently, David underwent intensive psychological counseling that included a thorough review by physicians of his biological parents' medical history. It was discovered that the CYS files on David contained information that both his biological parents had a history of mental illness.

On April 11, 1991, Appellants filed a complaint against CYS alleging fraud and negligent infliction of emotional distress for CYS's failure to inform Appellants about the mental illness of David's natural parents, along with indications of their alleged drug abuse and alcoholism. After filing preliminary objections to Appellants' complaint that were denied, CYS, on January 11, 1993, filed an answer and new matter, to which Appellants filed a reply on January 21, 1993. Subsequently, on May 4, 1994, CYS filed a motion for judgment on the pleadings, which Common Pleas granted by order dated August 25, 1994. This appeal followed.

<u>IN THE COURT OF COMMON PLEAS OF LEHIGH COUNTY, PENNSYLVANIA</u>

<u>CIVIL ACTION - LAW</u>

THEODORE       and GLORIA   )
      as Parents and      )
Natural Guardians of DAVID  )
     and THEODORE and    )
GLORIA      Individually, )
                  )
     Plaintiffs       )
                  )   No. 90-C-3471
      vs.         )
                  )
LEHIGH COUNTY OFFICE OF    )
CHILDREN AND YOUTH SERVICES, )
                  )
     Defendant        )


THEODORE       and GLORIA   )
      as Parents and      )
Natural Guardians of DAVID  )
     and THEODORE and    )
GLORIA     , Individually, )
                  )
     Plaintiffs       )
                  )
      vs.         )   No. 91-C-1869
                  )
FAMILY AND COUNSELING      )
SERVICES, Formerly known as )
FAMILY AND CHILDREN'S SERVICE )
OF LEHIGH COUNTY,        )
                  )
     Defendant        )

<u>ORDER</u>

NOW, this   24ᵗʰ   day of August, 1994, following

the entry of written Briefs and oral Argument,

IT IS ORDERED that the Motion for Judgment on the Pleadings filed by the Defendant, Lehigh County Office of Children and Youth Services, is granted.[1]

BY THE COURT:

Robert K. Young, Judge

---

[1] In *Petula v. Mellody*, 138 Pa.Commw. 411, 631 A.2d 762 (1993), it was held that a local agency is only subject to liability for negligent acts. "Moreover, Section 8550, 42 Pa.C.S. §8550, does not create an exception to Section 8542 and as a result, does not permit the imposition of liability on a local agency for the willful misconduct of its employees." *City of Philadelphia v. Glim*, 149 Pa.Commw. 491, 613 A.2d 613 (1992). Plaintiffs' Counsel is correct in noting that in *Gibbs v. Ernst*, Nos. 1363 C.D. 1991, (Pa.Commw. Ct. August 20, 1992), it would appear that the local agency remains a party to that action, but there is no discussion regarding immunity and thus no indication that that issue was raised. In view of the plain language of *Petula*, the Court is of the opinion that the instant motion must be granted. *See also Capriglione, et al. v. County of Lehigh, et al.*, Lehigh County Case No. 93-C-2510.

---

The Commonwealth Court affirmed my grant of a Motion for Summary Judgment in favor of the Office of Children and Youth Services, on the basis that OCYS was protected by the "Sovereign Immunity Act". There are sound reasons for limiting the liability of governments and their agencies, but can you imagine having a child you have adopted setting your home on fire!

# PRODUCTS LIABILITY: SNYDER VS. FRUEHAUF

The Snyder cement bulk hauler lawsuit is the next case. Liability was based on the theory that the pressure vessel was built with a defective top hatch. These Product Liability cases constitute a significant part of a trial judge's work. They normally deal with the propriety of warning labels and lack of adequate safety shields as in the prior Bollinger fingers in the printing press case. The admissible evidence differs from ordinary negligence suits, in that the manufacturer of the product is permitted to produce expert testimony that the item met the state of the art regarding safety at the time of manufacture.

IN THE COURT OF COMMON PLEAS OF LEHIGH COUNTY, PENNSYLVANIA
CIVIL ACTION - LAW

BRIAN SNYDER and )
DENISE SNYDER, his wife, )
)
            Plaintiffs )
) No. 80-C-1121
        vs. )
)
FRUEHAUF CORPORATION,. )
)
            Defendant )

                    *    *    *    *    *

APPEARANCES:

        DWIGHT L. DANSER, ESQUIRE,

        PHILIP D. LAUER, ESQUIRE,
        And with him, LAUER AND MONAHAN, P.C.,

            On behalf of the Plaintiffs.


        MORTON F. DALLER, ESQUIRE,
        And with him, RAWLE & HENDERSON,

            On behalf of the Defendant.


                    *    *    *    *    *

                        OPINION

ROBERT K. YOUNG, Judge.

        A Jury Trial was held to resolve this product

liability case on October 22, 1985 through October 28, 1985.

Judge David E. Mellenberg, now deceased, was the Trial

Judge. The date of the incident was April 6, 1978, over 15 years ago. The delay is largely attributable to the Official Court Stenographer, who left the service of this County and who was delinquent in her work. The Plaintiffs' Post Trial Motions were timely filed, and were briefed and argued shortly after the transcripts were received. On May 18, 1993 the Post Trial Motions were denied. That Order has been appealed, which necessitates this Opinion.

The Husband/Plaintiff was injured when he climbed on top of a large pressurized dry bulk cement trailer, which was designed and manufactured by the Defendant. Manholes are located on top of the trailer to permit its loading. These manholes are hinged, and held down by six "dog legs". In order to unload the dry cement, the interior of the trailer is pressurized with air, which then forces the cement out piping when a valve is opened at the rear of the trailer. The manholes must be securely closed in order for the pressure to be maintained.

The Plaintiff was attempting to unload his cargo from the rear valve on the date of the incident, but was unable to build up sufficient air pressure within the trailer's body. He climbed the nearby ladder where he could

-2-

see that one of the manholes was not properly sealed, so that pressure could not build up. He was injured when he tried to push down the manhole lid with his foot.

The 12-person jury found (10-2) that the Defendant's product was not defective in manufacture or design, and that, if there was such a defect, it was not the proximate cause of the Plaintiff's accident. Unexplainedly, the jury then continued to answer three other questions. By a vote of 8-3 it concluded that the warnings were adequate; by 8-2 that the failure to provide warnings was not the proximate cause of the accident; and by 7-5 that the Plaintiff assumed the risk of his own injury. The Trial Judge ruled that the above verdict constituted a decision in favor of the Defendant, and against the Plaintiff. The apparent reasoning of the Court was that when 5/6 of the jury found no defect and no proximate cause, the balance of the answers were merely informational. It made no difference whether or not only seven of the jurors believed that the Plaintiff had assumed the risk of his damages by using his foot to push down a partially pressurized manhole cover. If the product was not defective, the Defendant is not liable.

-3-

The Plaintiffs also complain that the Trial Court committed error in several of its evidentiary rulings. The first such complaint is that two of the Defendant's employees/supervisors were permitted to state that although they did not personally train the Plaintiff, it was the standard and customary policy of the company to warn all of its employees not to stand on top of the trailers. This testimony was relevant circumstantial evidence on the issue of assumption of the risk. In any event, because the jury found that there was no product defect, and no proximate cause, any evidence regarding the theory of Assumption of Risk, whether admissible or not, becomes moot, and no prejudice can be shown.

The Plaintiffs challenge the Trial Judge's decision that James Aicher was a qualified expert as to the matters about which he testified. That witness testified that he took courses in mechanical engineering and design drafting at the Chicago Technical College, and stress analysis courses from Penn State University. He worked for years as a design draftsman and became the chief engineer of the company's Uniontown plant. He was thoroughly cross-examined regarding his credentials. Trial Courts are

-4-

granted broad discretion in deciding what opinions are needed by jurors, and who may be sufficiently qualified to aid the jury in deciding technical matters which are beyond their normal knowledge. Ruzzi v. Butler Petroleum Co., 527 Pa. 1, 10 A. 2d 1 (1991). The weight to be given such testimony, based in large part upon the qualifications of an expert, is for the jury. These same principles apply to the Matters Complained of on Appeal Numbers 3 and 5.

The Plaintiffs further argue that the Trial Court improperly limited their cross examination of several of the Defendant's expert witnesses, who testified on direct examination that they were not aware of the failure of any other cast aluminum lids on Fruehauf trailers. The Court did not permit inquiry into whether or not those witnesses had ever heard of failures on any other makes of trailers. Such information was irrelevant, beyond the scope of the direct testimony, and admittedly outside the realm of the expert's knowledge.

The Court's Points for Charge No. 9, 12, 15 and 21 are objected to by the Plaintiff. The only way to decide whether or not a jury charge represents a fair and accurate statement of the law is to examine it in its totality.

-5-

_Noble C. Quandel Co. v. Slough Flooring, Inc._, 384 Pa. Super. 236, 558 A.2d 99 (1989). The Plaintiffs have failed to reproduce the entire charge, which makes fruitless any effort to review it as a whole. The Defendant's more than adequate Brief attempts to address the appropriateness of each of the above-noted points for charge, and the Court adopts that discussion as its own.

Lastly, the Court remains of the opinion that the verdict was substantiated by the evidence. If the Defendant's experts were found to be credible, there is ample testimony that the trailer and its top-loading manholes were adequately designed using proper materials. The jury could also have reasonably concluded that the stomping on the cover by the Plaintiff was the cause of the accident, and not any design or material flaws.

BY THE COURT:

_____
Robert K. Young, Judge

Dated: September _10_ , 1993

If you checked the dates in the Snyder case, you will see that it took over 15 years to bring that case to a close. There is no point now, in 2018, in chastising any person or persons, but Snyder demonstrates that unreasonable delay does happen in the court system. Years ago, the Pennsylvania Supreme Court instructed the Common Pleas Judges to report any cases that remained unfinished 90 days or more from the date they were removed from the judge's active list. I understand that the rule did have some limited success in moving older matters, but from follow up newspaper stories, it appears that a few judges simply kept their old cases on their desks and did not report them as inactive. At the end of 2015, there were 67 civil jury and non-jury cases over six years old (3.3%) of the cases pending in Lehigh County (Administrative Office of Pennsylvania Courts).

# LARA vs. Dorney Park Coaster Company

For twenty-seven years, the Dorney Park Coaster Company (Dorney) had as one of its attractions a quarter-mile long automobile race track, which was operated under a license to Lehigh Auto Racing Association (LARA). On October 4, 1986, Dorney notified LARA that the franchise would not be renewed. LARA later discovered, with the help of the local newspaper, that Dorney and the Township of South Whitehall, in which the park is located, had come to an omnibus agreement in settlement of several outstanding tax and other issues. One of the "other" issues concerned the desire of the Township to stop the noisy car races.

LARA promptly filed a Complaint in Equity, seeking an injunction to compel Dorney to renew LARA's license due to the interference by the Township with LARA's and Dorney's contractual relations. The racing season would need to start in April of 1987. A Hearing was held by me on March 23, 1987, and my Decree and Adjudication were filed four days later. I denied the request for an injunction on legal grounds that are not germane to the point now being made. Time was short, and so I certified the case ready for immediate appeal.

LARA appealed to the Superior Court. That court filed its Judgment on November 12, 1987. Not only was that useless due to the fact that the racing season was already over, but the Superior Court decided that the case should have been appealed to the Commonwealth Court. It relinquished jurisdiction and transferred the case to the Commonwealth Court. That court heard Argument on April 19, 1988 and handed down its Order affirming my March 27, 1987 Decree on June 6, 1988. A Fourteen-month delay for a decision in an Equity matter is hardly expeditious.

Coincidently, The Dorney Park Coaster Co. and I met again on the fields of justice. A homeowner neighbor adjacent to the amusement park filed an action in Equity, asking the Court to enjoin certain loud noises from an old wooden roller coaster. When he moved into that home, the coaster was already there. It seemed to me that being a "traveling judge," without any particular courtroom, I might as well meet with the parties at the site. I first stopped by at the nearest Radio Shack store and bought a hand-held sound meter. I also looked up the OSHA standards for safe noises in the workplace.

I announced that there would be a "settlement conference" at the Plaintiff's home, at which I would need to see both the Plaintiff and someone in authority from the park. Further, the coaster was to be in operation, with the normal full load of screaming people. The time for confrontation was picked. We were able to park our cars in the Plaintiff's driveway where he greeted us. The only thing to do was to walk back to the property line and listen. It was really loud. I forget the actual decibel reading on the meter as the coaster whizzed by, but it was well over the allowable threshold. But, it was intermittent.

The old argument that the noise was there when the Plaintiff moved in carries little weight in law. You don't get a license to create a nuisance. If it is so loud that it is unhealthy, a fix is necessary. The Park Manager made an offer that the Plaintiff accepted—the park would build a substantial, high fence designed to send the sound back where it came from. Case over.

Post Script: I still have that sound meter. I used it to measure the noise of the freight trains as they moved through the little Boroughs in our area. There are three street crossings spread along the length of Emmaus, each requiring four warning horn blasts. Because the engines are designed and used to pull the train from either end of the engine there is no real front, no "beep, beep, beeping" as if the train was moving backward. The horns blow both in the direction the train is moving and to the rear, doubling the noise. Do we need to know where the train has been?

# A BENCH TRIAL:
# ERIE INSURANCE VS. MCBRIDE

In the Erie Insurance Group matter following, you again get to view my work as a fact finder. It was a non-jury trial that did not hinge upon the law, but had to be resolved on what I believed happened. The insurance company brought the suit in Equity. It asked for a declaratory judgment ruling that the company did not have to defend the Plaintiff in a car accident case.

IN THE COURT OF COMMON PLEAS OF LEHIGH COUNTY, PENNSYLVANIA

CIVIL ACTION - EQUITY

ERIE INSURANCE GROUP    )
)
    vs.         )  No. 87-E-0095
)
GRACE McBRIDE        )

ORDER

NOW, this  10th  day of March, 1989, following two hearings and the entry of written briefs by both parties,

IT IS HEREBY ORDERED AND DECREED that declaratory judgment is granted in favor of the Plaintiff, Erie Insurance Group, and against the Defendant, Grace McBride, to the effect that the Plaintiff, Erie Insurance Group, does not owe the Defendant, Grace McBride, any underinsurance motorist coverage.[1]

BY THE COURT:

Robert K. Young, Judge

---

[1] On May 23, 1985, the Defendant, Grace McBride (Grace) was

CONTINUATION OF FOOTNOTE

---

injured in an automobile accident that occurred on Allentown Road, West Rockhill Township, Bucks County, Pennsylvania. At the time of the accident Grace was a passenger in a car driven by Frank Benetz. Sometime after the accident Grace entered into a settlement agreement with Frank Benetz in exchange for $100,000.00.

The tortfeasor, Frank Benetz, was a minor who had been served alcohol, allegedly to the point of visible intoxication, at the Red Barn Inn in Trumbauersville, Bucks County, Pennsylvania, on the night of the accident. Armed with this information, Grace filed an action against the bar pursuant to the Dram Shop Act of Pennsylvania. On July 16, 1987, while the action was pending, Pinetop Insurance Company, Red Barn Inn's insurer, went into receivership in the State of Illinois.

At the time of the accident and all times thereafter, Grace's father, Hugh McBride (Hugh), was a policyholder with the Plaintiff, Erie Insurance Group (Erie). On March 5, 1987 Grace made a demand for underinsurance motorist coverage to Erie. Due to the terms of Hugh McBride's Erie insurance policy Grace can only obtain coverage if she establishes that she was a resident of her father's household at the time of the accident. Under Reliance Life Ins. Co. v. Burgess, 112 F.2d 234 (1940), the burden of proof by a preponderance of the evidence falls upon Grace to demonstrate the affirmative fact that she was a resident of her father's household at the time of the accident. Averment No. 28 of her New Matter apparently acknowledges this duty. Upon a review of all of the testimony, this Court finds that Grace did not show that it is more probable than not that she was living at her father's home on May 23, 1985.

As in any court proceeding the credibility of the witnesses are at issue and the instant case has been decided largely on that basis. In this case, a father and daughter testified on different days, and were therefore unintentionally sequestered. They attempted to put forth

-2-

CONTINUATION OF FOOTNOTE

————————————

one credible version but, upon close review, their testimony reveals important inconsistencies and contradictions.

First, Kayelyse Gerhart, a nurse who interviewed Grace approximately one month after her accident, testified for the Plaintiff, Erie. She testified that on June 18, 1985, Grace, who was recuperating at her father's apartment, told her "that prior to her accident she was living on Ghost Mountain with the Pagans." (N.T. p. 6). Next, the Court heard Hugh McBride state that on and prior to May 23, 1985, his daughter, Grace, had lived with him "for eight to nine months." (N.T. p. 15). He also stated that she had her clothing there, took her meals there, and slept there. (N. T. pp. 15, 16). Upon further direct questioning about the Pagans and Ghost Mountain, Hugh stated, "Grace lived with me at all times. Since she was a little, since she was one hour old, one hour old, yes." (N.T. p. 16). On cross-examination, when confronted with Grace's statement to Erie that she had been living in Hatboro, Pennsylvania with a man from October 1984 to April of 1985, and was therefore not living with him, Hugh declared the statement to be incorrect; because "she's been always there (his apartment) when I come home from work." (N.T. p. 23). He also stated "she was there when I went to bed at night." (N.T. p. 23).

Grace McBride, however, told a somewhat conflicting version concerning her residence prior to the accident. Although naturally she stated that on the day of the accident, May 23, 1985, she was living with her father, she also testified that for approximately eight to nine months prior to April 2, 1985 she was living with a friend, Rick Molino. (N.T. pp. 4, 12). When questioned further about this living arrangement with Rick Molino, Grace gave what the Court believes were incredible answers. For instance, although she first stated she lived with Rick Molino, she later recanted this by saying "I was living in the apartment, (Rick Molino's) yes, but I used to come over -- all my stuff was over at my parents' place." (N.T. p. 13). When asked if she remembered telling an adjuster for Erie that she lived in the apartment with Molino she replied, "I'm not

-3-

CONTINUATION OF FOOTNOTE

---

disputing the fact that I was there." (N.T. p. 14). Instead, Grace would like the Court to believe that although she "was there", she slept at her parents' apartment each night and returned to Rick Molino's dwelling each morning. (N.T. p. 14). Yet, by her own admission, Grace did not have her own bedroom at her father's apartment. She stated she slept on a fold-down sofa bed in the living room. (N.T. p. 10). She did testify, however, that she kept a set of electric hair rollers and a change of clothes or nighclothes at Rick's apartment (N.T. p. 14). Further, the Court draws an adverse inference against Grace for failing to call Mr. Molino as a witness without putting forth any reason for his absence.

Grace would also have the Court believe that she moved back in to her parents' home completely by April 2, 1985, approximately six weeks prior to the accident, although as stated earlier she told Kayelese Gerhart that at the time of the accident she was "living on Ghost Mountain with the Pagans." (N.T. p. 6).

When cross-examined concerning the statement made to Kayelese Gerhart, Grace asserted that she does not remember making that statement because at that time she was under heavy medication and also had "an alcohol problem". (N.T. p. 8). Although this may be true, it is also true that at that time she had no motive to give a different answer. On June 18, 1985 there was no motive other than to tell the truth. Admissions against interest clearly and voluntarily made by a party ordinarily possess high evidentiary value. Louk v. Comm. Unemployment Compensation Bd. of Review, 72 Pa. Commw. Ct. 1, 455 A.2d 766 (1983).

Kayelese Gerhart was, and still is, an uninterested party. When Kayelese transcribed Grace's statement, Grace had not yet made a claim for underinsurance benefits. It was only after Grace realized that she needed to show she was a resident relative of her father's household that she contradicts the statement she gave to Kayelese Gerhart.

-4-

CONTINUATION OF FOOTNOTE

---

As stated earlier, the Court does not believe that Grace was living with her father on May 23, 1985. This conclusion has been deduced from the testimony given by Grace and Hugh McBride and statements offered by Grace shortly after the accident. It has long been the law in Pennsylvania that it is within the province of the trial judge, sitting without a jury, to judge the credibility of the witnesses and to weigh their testimony. Allegheny County v. Monzo, 509 Pa. 26, 500 A.2d 1096 (1985). Similarly, the findings of a chancellor in an equity action are entitled to particular weight in a case in which credibility of witnesses must be carefully evaluated because he has had an opportunity to hear them and observe their demeanor on the stand. Peugot Motors of America, Inc. v. Stout, 310 Pa. Super. Ct. 412, 456 A.2d 1002 (1983).

The Court is perplexed by the Plaintiff's vehement objection to the Court's Habeas Corpus Motion to call Grace McBride to testify in the present case. It is the law in Pennsylvania, as well as other states, that when the Court deems it necessary, it may call, on its own initiative, a witness that it believes will help shed light on the truth in any proceeding. Commonwealth v. Gerlach, 20 D. & C.2d 290, (1958) affd. 399 Pa. 74, 159 A.2d 915 (1960) (Judge sitting in equity without jury may call witness); Commonwealth v. Bready, 189 Pa. Super. 427, 150 A.2d 156 (1959) (an inherent power). That the trial court has inherent power to summon witnesses seems inevitably included in the holding of the United States Supreme Court in In Re Peterson, 253 U.S. 300, 309 (1920); Wigmore on Evidence §2485 p. 282; Travis v. Southern Pac. Co., 210 Col. App. 2d 410, 425, 26 Cal. Rptr. 700, 707-708 (1962) (Judge may call witnesses in both civil and criminal cases).

It is noted that none of the holdings in the cases cited above, or in any of the court's other research, limit the court's witness calling power to criminal cases only or where the court's witness is not a party, as is suggested in Plaintiff's brief.

-5-

CONTINUATION OF FOOTNOTE

---

Contrary to the belief of Plaintiff, it was to Plaintiff's advantage to have Grace testify. Only after hearing Grace's testimony was the Court able to detect the obvious inconsistencies mentioned earlier, not only within Grace's testimony, but especially between Grace's and her father's testimony. These inconsistencies enabled the Court to make a determination as to the credibility of the testifying witnesses. This determination would not have been possible without Grace McBride's testimony. This issue was eloquently addressed by Sir Edward Burke in his Report of Committee on Warren Hasting's Trial; 31 Parl. Hist. 348 (1794):

> It is the duty of the Judge to receive every offer of evidence, apparently material, suggested to him though the parties themselves through negligence, ignorance, or corrupt collusion, should not bring it forward. A judge is not placed in that high situation merely as a passive instrument of parties. He has a duty of his own, independent of them, and that duty is to investigate the truth.

What was somewhat special about the Erie case was that I called my own witness. That is not a popular thing to do. The lawyers have their own plans about how to present a case. But I was the fact-finder, and believed that I needed more of them. Note the strong language above of Sir Edward Burke, set down in an English Court in 1794. Now that's precedent.

# A Shocking Jury Verdict

There was only one decision by a jury that shocked me. The nullification verdict that we reviewed a while ago was more than interesting, but in Veno—you will see my problem.

IN THE COURT OF COMMON PLEAS OF LEHIGH COUNTY, PENNSYLVANIA

CIVIL DIVISION - LAW

| | |
|---|---|
| CARL A. VENO, | ) |
| Plaintiff | ) |
| | ) |
| vs. | ) No. 83-C-3378 |
| | ) |
| HOWARD BLOCH, | ) |
| Defendant | ) |

ORDER

NOW, this 25ᵗʰ day of July , 1988, after the transcription and review of the relevant Notes of Testimony, oral argument, and entry of written briefs, the Plaintiff's Motion for New Trial on the issue of damages only is granted.[1]

BY THE COURT:

_Robert K. Young_
Robert K. Young, Judge

---

[1] Carl A. Veno, then a 50-year-old newspaper editor and former nominee for a Pulitzer Prize, was on Sunday evening of December 5, 1982 driving his Volkswagen in the City of Allentown. He entered one of that city's main intersections at Hamilton and Fifteenth Streets under the protection of a

CONTINUATION OF FOOTNOTE

---

green light. As he proceeded northwardly on Fifteenth Street and across Hamilton Street his car was struck at the left (driver's side) rear bumper by the automobile of the defendant. This brief synopsis of the accident is sufficient in view of the fact that following a trial the jury specifically found by a special interrogatory that the defendant was 100% negligent, there being no contributory negligence on the part of the plaintiff.

There is certainly no need to put again the issue of negligence before a jury. The defendant testified that as he saw the plaintiff's yellow light he "had begun [his] turn to go on to 15th Street" (N.T., p. 650). "I had made like maybe two-thirds of my turn, and then I had seen another car alongside of me." (N.T., p. 653). "I was trying to move away from his car, and I guess, I don't know if the other car was wacked or what, but he went with me when I was turning away from me, from him, and this, my front bumper, like I would say, this one edge here got like the rear passenger fender well of his car... . And basically it was not like a direct blow. It was more like a lance (sic) blow, like that. And, and the car was hit like right at the back tire. And that's one of the tires that was moving. And the car spun clockwise and, it ended up basically in the middle of these two, these two lanes right here." (N.T., p. 655).

The above statements taken together with the plaintiff's testimony that he was proceeding on a green light are completely sufficient to substantiate the issue of liability as decided by the jury. At the new trial, the defendant may of course bring out the facts of the collision as they relate to the severity of the contact between the automobiles and the nature and extent of the plaintiff's injuries.

Immediately following the accident, the plaintiff was transported to the hospital where he was placed in the intensive care unit for a period of four or five days. (N.T., p. 337). He was released from the hospital on December 18, 1982, 13 days after the accident, but continued

-2-

CONTINUATION OF FOOTNOTE

---

to be treated by several physicians long after his discharge. At the trial Mr. Veno called four medical witnesses, all of whom were his treating doctors, not experts brought in for the purpose of answering hypothetical inquiries.

Dr. Arthur A. Katz, a clinical psychologist whose qualifications were not challenged by the defendant, testified that after administering a series of four widely recognized psychological tests (Wechsler, Minnesota Multiphasic Personality Inventory, Rorschach, and Bender-Gestalt), it was his opinion that Mr. Veno evidenced "psychotic depression" tied to a "... trauma or some event in his life which led to this disability." (N.T., pp. 120-121). The symptoms of his malady were described by Dr. Katz as being "... depression that's beyond any level of reality ... the person had strange ideas, extreme incuriosity, and suicidal thoughts ... psychotic depression would be considered the highest depression, the far end of depression where the person can't function, they can't think." (N.T., pp. 107, 108, 113). Dr. Katz further testified that because of Mr. Veno's severe depression " ... any kind of activity that would require concentration or attention or attendance or scheduling, following through on work, would be difficult to do," and that his depression "... severely affect(s) his ability to interact with other people." (N.T., p. 142).

Dr. William W. Frailey, Jr. also testified. He examined Mr. Veno at the hospital on the date of the accident and diagnosed a concussion as a result of the accident. (N.T., p. 220). Without detailing all of Dr. Frailey's testimony, he concluded, in consultation with Dr. Robert Jaeger, that Mr. Veno suffered from post-concussive tinnitus (a constant ringing in the ears). Headaches also persisted, and as of June 6, 1983, six months after the accident, Dr. Frailey had still not discharged Mr. Veno to return to work. (N.T., p. 231). There were also continuing complaints of left-sided weakness. (N.T., p. 231).

Dr. Daniel Goldfarb (Board Certified by the American Board

CONTINUATION OF FOOTNOTE

———————————————

of Psychiatry and Neurology) saw Mr. Veno over 45 times during 1983-84. Dr. Goldfarb referred Mr. Veno to Dr. Secunda for a second opinion, which was that Mr. Veno was suffering from "... a post-traumatic stress disorder, major depression, and organic brain disorder." (N.T., p. 272). Dr. Goldfarb described Mr. Veno's symptoms as "... classic symptoms of major depressive disorders"; and diagosed Mr. Veno as having a "... major depressive disorder." (N.T., pp. 262-265).

Further, Mr. Veno produced the testimony of Dr. Steven R. Shore (Board Certified in Internal Medicine), who had seen Mr. Veno on December 15, 1982, only ten days after the accident and while he was stil in the hospital. Dr. Shore indicated his belief that the left-sided weakness was caused by the automobile accident (N.T., pp. 471-472), and that, as of the trial date over three years later, Mr. Veno remained disabled and could not be gainfully employed. (N.T., p. 475).

In addition to the above-noted medical testimony, Mr. Veno called Mr. Mark Lukas, the director of Hoover Rehabilitation Services who testified that Mr. Veno was not employable at the time of the July 7, 1986 trial. Dr. Andrew G. Verzilli, Professor of Economics at Drexel University also testified as to Mr. Veno's past and future loss of earnings, which at a <u>minimum</u> amounted to $25,000.00 <u>and</u> $77,000.00, respectively.

The defendant produced no medical witness, nor any witnesses to rebut Dr. Verzilli's evidence concerning past and future earning losses, nor did the defense call anyone to challenge the conclusions of Mr. Lukas regarding the lack of employability of the plaintiff. The jury awarded $4,000.00 for the non-economic damages and only $1,000.00 for loss of earnings. This was clearly against the weight of the evidence. The trial court is convinced that the jury took a personal dislike to the plaintiff. This probably occurred because Mr. Veno, whose complaint is that he now suffers from psychotic depression, exhibited a disinterested and extremely negative personality on the stand and during

-4-

CONTINUATION OF FOOTNOTE

---

the trial.

Throughout the trial Mr. Veno slumped in his chair and stared at the counsel table or the floor. He avoided all eye contact. At one point during his testimony, he indicated a need to regurgitate, and a wastebasket was quickly provided, although not actually used. When on the stand, his answers were given in a dull and seemingly unconcerned manner. The very symptoms of his condition caused a loss of ability to adequately present his case.

The plaintiff's treating physicians testified that the accident was the cause of the depression. There was no medical evidence to the contrary. While it is true that the plaintiff's life prior to the collision contained other misfortunes, the defendant has always been held legally responsible for the full measure of damages inflicted upon individuals in a weakened condition. See Heck v. Beryllium Corporation, 424 Pa. 140, 226 A.2d 87 (1966) citing with approval Restatement of Torts 2d, §461 (1965), and Offensend v. Atlantic Refining Company, 322 Pa. 399, 403, 185 A. 745, 747 (1936). There should be no distinction as to the amount of compensatory damages due a victim with a frail jaw bone or one with an infirm mentality.

Defense counsel calls the Court's attention to Boggavarapu v. Ponist, ___ Pa. ___, ___ A.2d ___ (filed May 20, 1988). In that case the plaintiff was bitten by his neighbor's dog, which required treatment with a band-aid and two Tetanus shots. The plaintiff received only his out-of-pocket medical expenses ($42.60) and nothing for pain and suffering. The Supreme Court of this Commonwealth refused to uphold the grant of a new trial, holding that the jury might well have believed that the two injections were merely "transient rub(s) of life and living, a momentary stab of fear and pain, or neither." However, in Boggavarapu, the alleged pains came from the tetanus needles, not the dog bite. The jury "found a tort in the dog bite, but found no pain because the pain alleged was the needle, and not the dog. A tortfeasor is not obliged to answer for what he did not cause simply because he is a tortfeaser." The

-5-

CONTINUATION OF FOOTNOTE

---

co-defendant hospital was found not negligent. Such is not the case at bar. There is no co-defendant. The only evidence adduced at Mr. Veno's trial was that the negligence of the defendant caused the motor vehicle accident which caused his "post traumatic stress disorder, major depression, and organic brain disorder." (infra).

In Cree v. Horn, ___ Pa. Super. ___, 539 A.2d 446 (1988) the Court upheld the trial court in refusing to grant a new trial on the issue of the adequacy of jury-awarded damages, and noted:

> "Where the trial court grants a new trial on the ground of inadequacy the appellate courts will not interfere in the absence of a gross abuse of discretion ... When the trial court refuses relief against an allegedly inadequate verdict the appellate court will exercise even greater caution in reviewing its action." Obviously, the function of determining whether a jury's verdict is arbitrary and capricious lies with the trial court, and its decision will not be set aside in the absence of clear error of law or palpable abuse of discretion.

Bronchak v. Rebmann, 263 Pa. Super. 136, 140, 397 A.2d 438, 440 (1979) (emphasis in orginal), quoting, Paustenbaugh v. Ward Baking Co., 374 Pa. 418, 421-21, 97 A.2d 816, 818 (1953).

In Cree the jury awarded $10,000.00 to each of the plaintiffs as "other damages". No past or future earning losses were given. Unlike Mr. Veno's trial, there was considerable evidence produced by the defendants' medical experts. The jury in Cree was provided with credible testimony on both sides of the issue of damages, which was not present in this trial. As noted in Cree "Because the record fully supports the determination that appellee's

CONTINUATION OF FOOTNOTE

———————————————————————

negligence did not cause the alleged damages, we find nothing shocking in the verdict of the jury." 539 A.2d, at 449.

This trial court finds it shocking to compensate Mr. Veno with the sum of $1,000.00 for the unrefuted serious economic consequences to him as a result of the clear negligence of the operator of a motor vehicle. Mr. Veno's negative trial demeanor is difficult to adequately describe. The jury's award, in light of the only evidence before it, indicates a capricious and arbitrary disregard of the facts, and, we believe, was due to the plaintiff's unpleasantness during the trial, which is the essence of his malady. If this verdict is permitted to stand, it will encourage the disallowance of the claims or defenses of any litigant with a personality characteristic that improperly happens to be out of favor with the jury. A jury must disregard sympathy or antipathy, and base its verdict solidly upon the facts presented to it.

The panel of the Superior Court affirmed my Order in a split decision—two to one.

# A SHORT EXPLANATION OF POST TRIAL RELIEF

After a trial, the lawyers fairly often made requests for "Post Trial Relief." They may be seeking an expedited appeal, a new trial, to assess interest, to award counsel fees, to poll the jury, etc. In the next case, the Defendants asked for a new trial. My footnote did not cover one point that they raised. I have included here the short Opinion issued to address that item as it may enlighten you about the fact that some lawsuits are not at all glamorous, but can become long and tedious. Note the number of exhibits sent out with the jury.

And, I just could not resist telling you that about six months after the trial, Mr. Grossinger, AKA Dr. Jerome Grossinger, who I had just ruled against, was the doctor to whom I was referred to perform a root canal operation on me. He did a fine job, but I did suffer some pre-operation anxiety.

IN THE COURT OF COMMON PLEAS OF LEHIGH COUNTY, PENNSYLVANIA

CIVIL ACTION - LAW

EDGAR CONSTRUCTION CO., INC.,   )
                           )
        Plaintiff         )
                           )
        vs.             )  No. 87-C-1454
                           )  No. 88-C-816
JEROME GROSSINGER and      )
LEILA GROSSINGER,        )
                           )
        Defendants      )

\*    \*    \*    \*    \*

APPEARANCES:

      ERV D. McLAIN, ESQUIRE,
        On behalf of the Plaintiff.

      KEVIN T. FOGERTY, ESQUIRE,
      And with him, BLANK, ROME, COMISKY & McCAULEY,
        On behalf of the Defendants.

\*    \*    \*    \*    \*

OPINION

ROBERT K. YOUNG, J.

The Court adopts as its Opinion the five-page footnote appended to its April 22, 1994 Order. That Order, which is the subject of this Appeal, denied the Defendants' Motion for Post Trial Relief. The Court's footnote does not, however, address one of the issues raised by the

Defendants, which is the Court's rejection of the Defendants' request to itemize each element of damages within the Verdict Slip.  There were approximately 29 separate items, some of which were withdrawn during the trial.  The jury took with it into the deliberation room over 50 exhibits, including correspondence, work orders, proposals, charts, change orders, credit memorandums, and drawings, plus 45 photographs.  The Court used its discretion in deciding that the use of Pa.R.C.P. 1513 was not appropriate.  Any Special Fact Interrogatories would have been numerous and confusing, particularly when coupled with various admitted credits.  The jury had heard all of the conflicting testimony and was well able to decide which items of damages were justly due to the Plaintiff, and which ones were not.

BY THE COURT:

Robert K. Young, Judge

Dated: July 1 , 1994

-2-

I have removed some cases that I thought were pretty interesting, because in reviewing the whole manuscript, it came to me that what I might enjoy rereading, could come across as too academic and redundant. By this time in the book, you will have at least scanned court cases that fell under the jurisdiction of each of the five Divisions of Pennsylvania's Court of Common

Pleas. Probably because I disliked most of the work in Family Court, it has somehow occurred that the last case deals in that area. You will miss some reality about what a trial judge puts up with if you skip it. I think you will agree that it takes a lot of judicial restraint and patience to handle some parents.

<u>IN THE COURT OF COMMON PLEAS OF LEHIGH COUNTY, PENNSYLVANIA</u>

<u>CIVIL ACTION - LAW</u>

LOUIS E.                              )
                                      )
        Plaintiff                     )
                                      )
        vs.                           )   No. 83-C-918
                                      )   No. 55 PHL 85
BONNIE P.                             )
                                      )
        Defendant                     )

                    *    *    *    *    *

APPEARANCES:

        W. THOMAS ANTHONY, JR., ESQUIRE,
            On behalf of the Plaintiff.

        GWIN M. KROUSE, ESQUIRE,
            And with her, BROWN, BROWN,
              SOLT, WIENER & KROUSE,
            On behalf of the Defendant.


                    *    *    *    *    *


                <u>MEMORANDUM OPINION</u>

ROBERT K. YOUNG, Judge.

        A full evidentiary Hearing was held in this matter

on October 10, 1984.  On December 7, 1984, as a result of

that Hearing, this Court issued a custody and visitation schedule which was to be implemented and followed by the parties.  Since that ORDER the Defendant has retained new counsel.  The Defendant appealed this Court's ORDER to the Pennsylvania Superior Court on January 3, 1985.  Hence this Memorandum Opinion.

The parties to this action are presently separated husband and wife.  There were two children born of their marriage, C_____ and M_____, who were three and five years old at the time of the Hearing.

On the date of the Hearing, Bonnie _____ lived in an apartment in Fountain Hill, Bethlehem, Lehigh County, Pennsylvania, with the two children.  She testified that she changed her residence yearly.  She was an unemployed data processing student at the Lehigh County Community College. She received Public Assistance in an amount of three hundred fifty-five dollars ($355.00) each month, and her husband was paying support to her in an amount of seventy-two dollars ($72.00) each week.

After the parties had separated, sometime early in 1983, they had arranged a visitation schedule.  Under that arrangment Bonnie _____ allowed her husband to exercise visitation overnight on alternating weekends.  During the

-2-

intervening weeks she allowed her husband to visit the children on one weekday evening. These visits, by agreement took place in Bonnie '_____ home.

As a result of conversations between Bonnie _____ and her two children, Bonnie _____ unilaterally suspended visitation after April 1983. She believed that her husband had sexually molested C____, who was then two years old. The Defendant did not take C____ to a doctor at that time. Two months later, in June 1983 the Defendant consulted the Lehigh County Office of Children and Youth Services concerning her belief that the Plaintiff had sexually molested C____. That Office appointed Susan Maurer, an ongoing protective services worker with whom the Court is quite familiar, to investigate the mother's accusations.

Mrs. Maurer testified under a Court ORDER at the Hearing. Her investigation included an interview with C____, M____, and Bonnie _____, at Bonnie _____ home, as well as a second interview with C____ alone. Mrs. Maurer used anatomically correct dolls to assist C____ in articulating the events with which the Defendant was concerned. During the first interview, M____ often spoke for C____. M____ spoke in a manner which Mrs. Maurer

-3-

believed was beyond a five-year-old's comprehension. Mrs. Maurer believed that M._____ was expressing a transferral of her mother's beliefs. Mrs. Maurer filed a report on the allegations, which report classifed the accusation as "indicated". However, Mrs. Maurer candidly testified that all of the information she compiled indicated only that the alleged abuse possibly occurred. She adamantly stated that the evidence she possessed did not indicate any abuse beyond a reasonable doubt.

On March 5, 1984 Bonnie _____ allowed visitation to resume. The Defendant allowed her husband to visit their children, but only under the constant supervision of one Susan Zelco (who submitted a Report to the Court). In May 1984 Louis _____ asked to exercise overnight visitation with the children. The Defendant strenuously objected to that request.

On May 21, 1984 the Honorable Maxwell E. Davison ORDERED both parties to undergo counseling. Bonnie _____ did not comply with that ORDER. She testified that she had never seen that ORDER; that she did not need counseling; that she was not sick; and in any event that she was too busy to spend any time in counseling.

In July, 1984 Bonnie _____ and the two

-4-

children were living with Bonnie's parents. During that month Bonnie again lodged complaints accusing her husband of sexually abusing C____. At that time, she again unilaterally suspended visitation, which had not resumed as of the date of this Court's Hearing.

The Court met with both C____ and M____ **in camera.** As a result of that meeting we found that C____, a child only three years old, did not understand the nature of an oath. She did not comprehend the importance of telling the truth; nor did she understand the imprudence of telling a lie. In such a case, we cannot attach much, if any, import to her statements. We did conclude, though, that both children love their father, and miss him. They did not understand why their father was no longer a part of their lives.

The evidence introduced to this Court did not convince us that sexual abuse occurred. The only evidence in support of Bonnie____ accusations was hearsay statements of a two-year-old child. This Court cannot practically or prudently accept such evidence as dispositive of such a crucial issue, especially since the child did not comprehend the importance of telling the truth even one year later. However, as the accusations are of such a grave

-5-

nature, our ORDER, which is the subject of this appeal, has been framed in an attempt to preclude the father from having any opportunity to repeat the alleged acts.

This Court is convinced that the major problem in this case, as in many custody matters, is the antagonism between the parents. The Defendant's deep-seated hatred toward her husband has transcended her concern for the upbringing of their two children. This conclusion is supported by Bonnie _____ behavior since this Court's ORDER of December 7, 1984. She has denied Louis _____ visitation on every scheduled visit since this Court's ORDER. To make matters worse, at a recent contempt Hearing before this Court, the Defendant testified that she would never adhere to a Court ORDER which she did not believe was in her best interest.

The Court is aware of the important roles that both a mother and a father play in a child's life. It is not proper that two precocious, bright, healthy children such as C_____ and M_____ are being raised without any contact with their natural father. The Legislature has clearly mandated that both parents are to be allowed access to their children. Furthermore, both parents are responsible for the upbringing of their children, even after the bitterest of

-6-

separations.

23 Pa. C.S.A. 1002 provides:

> The General Assembly declares that it is the public policy of this Commonwealth, when in the best interest of the child or children, to assure a reasonable and continuing contact of such child or children with both parents after a separation or dissolution of marriage, and the sharing of the rights and responsibilities of child rearing by both parents.

From all of the evidence received by this Court, we are convinced that Louis _____ deeply loves and cares for his two children.  This affection is so strong that he has been willing to abide by the most rigorous restraints upon visitation which his wife and this Court have imposed.  He has passively tolerated outrageous behavior and restrictions in order to shield his two children from the harsh side effects of a separation.

For all of the foregoing reasons, we believe that this Court's ORDER of December 7, 1984 is in the best interests of the two minor children involved, and will best promote this Commonwealth's public policy of assuring reasonable and continuing contact between the _____ children and both of their parents.  We believe that this Court's ORDER will also adequately protect those children from the improbable dangers raised by the Defendant.

Further, on behalf of the children, who have visited with their father only once to our knowledge for almost a year, we urge an expedited review of our Order of December 7, 1984, particularly in view of the Supersedeas granted to the mother.

BY THE COURT:

Robert K. Young, Judge

Dated: June 7ᵗʰ, 1985.

IN THE COURT OF COMMON PLEAS OF LEHIGH COUNTY, PENNSYLVANIA

CIVIL ACTION - LAW

LOUIS                              )
                                   )
          Plaintiff                )
                                   )
     vs.                           )   No. 83-C-918
                                   )
BONNIE                             )
                                   )
          Defendant                )

MODIFICATION ORDER

AND NOW, this _____ day of February, 1986, following the appearance in person of the Defendant before this Court, the prior Orders of December 7, 1984 and October 18, 1985 are hereby modified as follows:

1.  The body attachment issued in the second paragraph of the October 18, 1985 Order is dissolved, with the costs of filing being placed on the Defendant.

2.  A contempt hearing will be scheduled by this Court at a convenient time by separate memorandum relating to the Defendant's possible disobedience of the Custody Order of December 7, 1984.

3. The Order of Custody issued on December 7, 1984 shall be modified as follows, with the below paragraph letters corresponding to the paragraph letters of the aforesaid Order:

(c) The father's first visitation shall be on January 30, 1985 from the hours of 5:00 p.m. to 7:00 p.m. so that the children can slowly become reacquainted. The father's next visit shall be on either the 8th or 9th of February, at the father's choice, between the hours of 9:00 a.m. until 6:00 p.m. From then on the schedule set forth in paragraph (c) of the underlying Order shall take effect.

(f) The Court intended that the visitations should be in the continuous presence of at least one of the father's parents, including the periods of transportation. Further, the word presence shall mean being in the same room, not merely the same house. The father shall pick up and deliver the children at the home of the mother's parents.

Those portions of the Order of December 7, 1984 which have not been specifically modified by this Order shall remain in full effect until further Order.

4. The mother shall not remove either or both of

-2-

the children from the Commonwealth of Pennsylvania without prior Order of Court, excepting only that she may take them on short vacations to the Atlantic seashore if these vacations do not interfere with the father's visitations.

5. In view of the past conduct of the mother, and without making a finding of contempt at this time, the Court orders Bonnie _____ to post a performance bond in the amount of Ten Thousand Dollars ($10,000.00) to be drawn to the benefit of the Commonwealth of Pennsylvania, conditioned upon her obeyance of every obligation placed upon her by the Order of this Court of December 7, 1984 as modified by this Order. In the first instance, Bonnie _____ is permitted to enter her own recognizance in the total amount of said Ten Thousand Dollars ($10,000.00). However, if she violates any of the conditions of the above-referenced Orders, the Court reserves the right to require posting by her of cash or other surety in lieu of her own recognizance.

BY THE COURT:

Robert K. Young, Judge

# CHILD SUPPORT:
# DOMESTIC RELATIONS SECTION CASES

Very often, a custody case is followed by a Petition for Support. When couples separate, with or without children, there are apt to be problems in maintaining the style of life for two households that existed while together.

I took my turn in Support Court, which is a branch of the Family Court Division as described in the diagram included in the beginning of the text. In any event, Support Court was for me a difficult assignment. A whole day was set aside periodically for just these cases. The courtroom was always packed at the beginning. It seemed to me that the women were almost always represented by counsel, but the men only occasionally.

As in criminal court, the clerical staff handled the files in tall piles. I, and they were seated, but the attorneys and clients stood in front of us. My recollection is that we all had the goal of at least 25 cases being resolved in the morning. Before the cases came to me, the County's Domestic Relations Section personnel had met at least with the plaintiff, and with the defendant if the issue was nonpayment of a Support Order. That department had dedicated people, doing a job that ended in pleasing hardly any of their clients.

The morning cases normally flowed along well, because they were intentionally the easiest ones. After I had listened to as many facts as were needed I was able to dictate a Support Order on the spot, based upon approved guidelines adjusted by the facts of each case. The same cannot be said for the afternoon crowd. Then we came to deal with complicated situations, but also with the recalcitrant males who were brought there to face a charge of Contempt of Court. If guilty of that, bad things could happen, and they knew it. It was not an accident that the most grievous offender was the first on the afternoon list. Those waiting in the courtroom paid attention to that one.

"That one," on one occasion, was a medical doctor, who was subject to a Support Order from another judge. The amounts of required support for his estranged wife and children were substantial, but in accordance with his earnings. I was informed that this was the third time that he had fallen behind, and that his delinquency was jeopardizing his children's education.

There is really no advantage in putting a debtor of any kind in jail. However, I had that crowd of onlookers looking on. My plan, not unusual, was to fine him and sentence him to a short term in prison, which I would immediately suspend. That way if he again missed a payment, the Sheriff could take him right to jail.

He was standing between the lawyers when with an appropriate frown I said that I found him in contempt of the Support Order, and that he was to pay a prescribed fine and serve time in the Lehigh County Prison...BAMM! He fainted right to the floor before I could finish the suspended sentence part. His wife's counsel was a former nurse and took charge of rousing him. We finished the Order later. I wonder what those other Defendants thought.

# JUDICIAL RESTRAINT

What a judge says from the bench or elsewhere, seems to carry more weight than is deserved. I learned to apply a good bit of judicial restraint in talking. One of the items covered at the National Judicial College was how to talk to the press. The advice was never to say, "no comment." A judge should always be able to at the least explain the procedural position of the case in which the reporter was interested—what was done, what was going to happen next. But, a judge should never try to explain his or her written decision. The judge said in that edict whatever he or she wanted to say. Amplification normally creates confusion and more questions.

Judges must be careful to whom they talk. There were at least three people I can think of that I could not politely ignore. They asked to see me and I obliged, but not alone. If you meet alone, the listener is able to misquote you with only your word against his or hers. Judge Maxwell Davison brought home the concept of judicial restraint one day by accident, I think. I was assigned to his courtroom and when I stepped up and into his empty chair, I could not miss a small but noticeable large-print note that only he could see while on the bench that read, MOUTH SHUT.

And in both thought and conversation, remember that a judge should not be judgmental. I have been surprised at the occasional insights into the situation that litigants reveal. Give everyone an equal opportunity to express themselves. Pre-judging a person or disputed issue is not smart nor fair.

Two other areas where verbal restraint is wise are (1) refraining from introducing humor into the proceedings, and (2) not declaring that an Order or Sentence is "sending a message." Sometimes humorous things happen in court, but as a general rule, the parties and lawyers see nothing funny in being in court. Judges must treat every individual equally under the circumstances. When it is announced that the judge is sending a message, it tells the public that the judge has done something special, that he or she has been extra hard on this Defendant or Party as a deterrence. That is not a judge's job.

The wearing of a judicial robe acts to restrain a person's behavior. My belief is that the robe is meant to depersonalize a judge. That is, the robe is a symbol of the theory that a party will get a fair hearing no matter who is wearing a robe. The public sees the person as a judge. Lawyers talk about "going to Court," not, "I am going to Judge X." In my opinion, United States Chief Justice Rehnquist erred by having large colorful stripes sewn on the shoulders of his robe because he admired the costume robe used in the Gilbert and Sullivan operetta *The Pirates of Penzance*. He only drew attention to himself. If you look up his name on the Internet, his latest two photographs show the chevrons.

# THE CASES I DISLIKED, THE CASES I LIKED

We near the end of my nostalgia trip into the products of the work I did as a trial judge, not taken just for my enjoyment, but to provide my Great-Grandchildren with some insight into what I was like. Next are the cases that I most disliked, a case about which I was neutral, and my favorite cases. Curiously, they each relate to the others.

My most emotional and unhappy cases involved Termination of Parental Rights. Who was I, who was anyone, to forever take a child away from its mother and father? I noticed that those cases were hard on the lawyers as well. The Office of Children and Youth attorneys were convinced that the child's needs and welfare were best met by the removal from the parents, leading to adoption some times. Counsel for the parents often truly believed that their clients just needed a little more time and training to solve their problems. Court-appointed Guardians usually worked strenuously to foster the child's future, and protect it from all sides, including me.

A Termination case that I will never forget, involved the mother, who was living alone in Slatington on public welfare with her very young child. The Office of Children and Youth Services was coordinating a variety of services to her, including visiting nurses to her home, caseworkers for advice, transportation, and psychological counseling. Following a lengthy Hearing, we all visited her first-floor apartment. The housing was clean and quite adequate for the use of mother and child. The mother tried to comply with all of the instructions given to her about the proper care of the baby. She was gentle. She held the child lovingly.

And now comes the "but." The mother was clearly mentally inadequate to raise any child. She sometimes forgot to feed him; to take him for walks; to bath him; to give him medication in the prescribed amounts or on time, or at all. Without the OCYS financial aid needed to hire a taxicab, she could not take the baby for his medical check-ups. The kitchen cooking stove was disconnected due to her forgetfulness in turning it off. The only way that she could safely keep the child was if OCYS would and could afford to provide constant daily help. Although the OCYS caseworkers made special efforts to provide many kinds of support to her, she still could not handle the job of caring for an infant.

Here we then were faced with a loving mother who was trying as hard as she could, but without the mental capacity to safely raise her child. Further, the medical psychologist testified that the mother's ability would not improve in the foreseeable future. I terminated her as a parent. She died of cancer a few years later.

A job that I thought might cause me some anxiety actually turned out to be neither a problem nor a pleasure. Following several legislative attempts, the Orphans' Court was charged with the obligation of discovering and deciding whether or not a young woman under the age of 18 fully understood the consequences and other options that she had before obtaining an abortion.

Well, that was going to require a Hearing if her parents would not consent or had not been told about the abortion. There was no precedent, at least in Pennsylvania, as to how to proceed. With the advice of my Administrative Counsel, Jan Thwaites, we decided that the Hearing would (a) be held in a quiet jury room (not our courtroom), (b) I would not wear a robe,

(c) there would be no Court Stenographer, but I would use that old tape recorder that you heard of earlier, (d) the Hearings would be held at 4:00 p. m. or thereabouts so that the minor, if in school, could attend without needing an excuse, (e) the minor could bring a friend with her, and (f) the record (a separate cassette tape) would be sealed.

The alternatives to an abortion available to a pregnant woman are limited. She can choose to raise the child, and if so, there may be social agencies or family members willing and able to help her. She can arrange for an adoption. My job was not to advise her about which choices to make, but to make sure that she understood them.

After Jan and I worked out the details of the required hearing, I made a call to the Allentown Diocese identifying myself and asked to see the Bishop for the purpose of discussing the new law and its implementation. In due course, I was answered by a Monsignor. We arranged a luncheon. I shared my thoughts on the subject. He expressed no opinions nor offered any suggestions, and thanked me for the meal. It was clear that the Roman Catholic Church intended to distance itself from the topic.

The Women's Center, Planned Parenthood and those few doctors who performed abortions were made aware of our procedure. A form Order was developed that I signed and gave to the expecting mother, in which I stated that a Hearing was held and that I found that the minor understood her options. The system, now known as a "By Pass" because it bypasses the woman's parents, seemed to work well. We had no complaints. How much good it accomplished is to me unknown, but I wish to believe that it did no harm.

# ADOPTIONS

And now, appropriately, following cases about parents having their children taken away and procedures relating to abortions, we turn to the happiest decisions—Adoptions.

There is no need for a long opinion or footnote in an Adoption. None of my Adoptions were ever appealed. There is a Hearing held with a full staff in attendance and a Court Stenographer. By the time of that event, the attorney on behalf of the adopting parents has already filed all of the required Consents, Petitions, Certificates and Reports. Everything has normally been reviewed before the Hearing. No one wants a continuance. Some adoptions are brought by the Office of Children and Youth Services following a Termination Decree or upon consent by a parent; some are brought by a stepparent, others by a private adoption agency.

One Petition for Adoption was brought by a sixty-year old woman asking to adopt a forty-year old non-relative companion. That called for some explanation. She frankly testified that she was so fond of the adoptee that she had included her as the main beneficiary of her estate. The adoption would greatly reduce the inheritance taxes, as she would now be making a bequest to her legal daughter. Why not?

Final Adoption Hearings were held in a bright jury room next to my office. I do not remember an unpleasant adoption. Everyone sat around the jury table. The attorney asked standard questions for the record, always one about the child's name henceforth. That information was needed for a new birth certificate that was to be issued shortly. Depending upon the ages of the adopting parents and whether they had other children, the attorney might ask if they understood the responsibilities and irrevocable nature of an adoption. I sometimes chimed in at the end to ask them to consider, and not decide right away, the issue of when, if ever, to tell the child about the adoption.

I did wear a robe at adoptions. It was an important and serious event, with long-term consequences. Secondly, when young children were being adopted, which was most of the time, my Court Crier took an instant Polaroid photograph of the new parents and child. (My Great-Grandchildren may have no idea what a Polaroid photograph is!) Time after time, in spite of my protestations, the couple wanted me in the photo. With a robe, I knew that in later years I would not be mistakenly thought to be the adopting father. After all, I have five children of my own.

# AFTERTHOUGHTS

The task of describing what it was like to be a Pennsylvania Trial Judge has been set out in the main text. At this point, it seems to me that I ought to share some of what I believe I learned from the experience.

One of the most important conclusions is that the Court System (not just the judges) is continually working at protecting those rights enumerated within the first Ten Amendments of the Constitution (The Bill of Rights) and the Fourteenth Amendment (Due Process and Equal Protection). Even the Declaration of Independence was brought into the case of Barbara vs. Matchmaker. In M. K., the Superior Court confirmed its mindfulness that "…freedom from unwarranted governmental intrusion is a basic right which is protected by the Fourteenth Amendment." Whole categories of legal issues, including "Right to Die," Termination of Parental Rights, Electric Shock Treatment and Bypass Hearings require Court review, with some requiring findings by clear and convincing evidence. The concept of Due Process is tightly woven into the protective blanket of the law.

Voting rights are specifically protected under the 15th, 19th, 24th, and 26th Amendments. Also, recall my use of a written Colloquy before accepting a Guilty Plea, the Robinson case issues of shackles, plus the new Supreme Court ruling that a death sentence to a minor constitutes a cruel and unusual punishment.

The Courts also protect Governments—from the people! The Governmental Immunity cases I reported were supported by precedents and statutes that will not, in certain circumstances, permit individuals or groups that have been injured by government agencies to collect sums of money from the public treasury. Remember the Office of Children and Youth Services incident with the adoptee setting fire to the adoptive parent's house, and remember the Bollinger daughter having her fingers cut by a School District's unshielded printing press.

Further, the Courts are sometimes required to protect the rights of one Government against another Government, such as in Olhanoski, where PennDOT tried to tag the Borough of Emmaus with liability to an injured worker.

In a strange way, the Courts often protect the people from themselves. Why is the jury prohibited from being told about a party's insurance? Because the judges have observed that juries lose their objectivity when they learn that an insurance company will be paying the bill (seemingly not considering that an overly generous award will probably result in an increase of premiums for all policy holders).

Regarding the Courts' protection of the people from themselves, much more important are the rare but critical times when majorities use customs, ordinances and laws to oppress minorities. I do not think that history will rate the courts performance in that area very highly. Differences in race and religion, which should strengthen us, should be faced with the indifference that every judge needs to apply to all matters that he or she is assigned to resolve.

The wisdom or luck of our Judicial System transcends the proven ability to settle most of society's internal arguments. Thanks to Chief Justice John Marshall and the acquiescence of our first leaders in government, the Courts have been able to protect the three branches of Government from each other.

They decide whether the Executive Branch or the Legislative Branch are violating the Constitution, and even decide whether their own prior decisions have been proven wrong.

The whole System is held together by "Checks and Balances." The Checks are much easier to see. They usually surface as a "no" or "stop." It is the balancing of competing rights and obligations that cause the frictions, the heat of which needs thoughtful cooling. Considering the diversity in ethnicity and religions of our population, the system of justice in the United States is nearly miraculous.

I thought the schematic chart near the beginning of the book might be helpful in understanding the scope of the court in which I sat. I am, near the end, suggesting a humorous semi-analogy concerning the balance of powers that exists among and between the three branches of government.

In my youth (and even lately when visiting with my children) it was fun and yet stressful to engage each other with the quick hand-game of Rock, Scissors, and Paper. Imagine the part of the Paper being the Congress, producing lots of laws. The Scissors, able to cut through many of those laws by Special Orders, representing the Executive, and of course the inflexible Rock is the Supreme Court.

Now in the real game there are two players (today perhaps the Democrats and Republicans). At the simultaneous throw of hands there is either a tie or someone overcomes the other. The Paper over the Rock; the Rock smashing the Scissors, or the Scissors cutting the Paper. Thus, all are equal in power.

In real life, the Paper Congress and Scissor Executive can indeed stymie each other. But, since the Supreme Court does not entertain lawsuit against itself, that old Rock is very hard to move. In the past, it has taken constitutional amendments, or the slow self-enlightenment of the Court itself.

So, as I and many others see it, the Court System is nonsensically "first among equals." And that's the way it should be. Can you imagine the President and Executive Branch with all of its Agencies being the ultimate "Deciders?" Would you rather have our Two-Branch Congress of over six hundred Representatives and Senators take complete charge "with the consent and advice" of the other two "equals?" Please say no.

# A Point for Charge
# for my Great-Grandchildren

Iknow that earlier I decried the "sending of messages" by judges. But that was when we were "on the Bench." Now, at the end of my lengthy job description, I have a point for charge to pass on to my Great-Grandchildren—to all Great-Grandchildren.

The generations of men and women who have proceeded you are soon to transfer to you an intricate, working and successful system of justice. It has been shaped by the trials and tribulations of millions of people from all races and nations. Traces of the concepts it holds reach back thousands of years, and yet it serves mankind today. It affords everyone a fair chance at obtaining the pursuit of happiness promised to us in our nation's Declaration of Independence. I hope by reading this book you will have learned to appreciate how the entire Court System is necessary for the day by day implementation of the due processes guaranteed by the Bill of Rights and Fourteenth Amendment, and in this understanding, I charge you to become well-informed citizens, willing to contribute to your community's general welfare under the rule of law.

And in your time on our planet, try to calm the relationships between our many political and ethnic sub groups. Always support and have confidence in the amazing system of justice that I have tried to describe to you.

To my Great-Grandchildren-
　　May you be useful, kind and happy.

To the curious people-
　　Keep your minds well open, and your mouths mostly shut.
　　　　　Bob Young, Great-Grandfather
　　　　　Retired Trial Judge

# BIOGRAPHICAL NOTE ABOUT THE AUTHOR

The book in your hands is not a biography. It is a memoir of the eleven and a half year period of my life spent as a Common Pleas Court Judge. I endeavored to describe the job of a county trial judge to my Great-Grandchildren. I also hope that others, especially students interested in becoming lawyers, will find it interesting and informative. My wife, Carolyn, who reads a lot, tells me that most people like to know something personal about authors. "It's traditional," she says.

I was born in March of 1931, and was the second child of intelligent, caring, and economically stable parents. They believed in a good education. I attended Germantown Friends and Sidwell Friends Schools and graduated from Westtown Friends School, Haverford College and the University of Pennsylvania Law School.

I opened a law office in Lehigh County, where after a period of handling almost every kind of legal issue, I narrowed the balance of my 27 years in the profession to the three specialized areas of real estate transactions, wills and decedents' estates, and municipal law.

I served as solicitor for a Borough, a Township, a Community College and a Vocational/Technical School. I also served as a board member of a school district, the Lehigh County Red Cross, a Chamber of Commerce, the Industrial Development Corporation, the Joint County Planning Commission, the Lehigh County Charter Commission and the Minsi Trails Council of the Boy Scouts of America. I was a scoutmaster and volunteered for several community endeavors for local public parks and historical societies.

Mrs. Young and I have been married for 66 years, living in the same home for sixty of those years. Our five children are college graduates—three of them holding various graduate degrees. Life has been good to us.

# ACKNOWLEDGEMENTS

My Parents Dr. Donald R. and Ada W. Young

Your Great-Grandmother Carolyn E. Young

Our Five Children, Donald, David, William, Paul and Nancy (Without whose cooperation there would be no Grand or Great-Grandchildren)

Long-term Secretary, Barbara A. Yost

Counsel to the Orphans' Court, Jan Thwaites

The Senior Deputy Attorney General, Larry Barth

Lehigh County Court Criers and Tipstaffs

    Michael Brocshack

    Jack Parks

    Edie Schwoyer

    Robert Ring

Peter M.G. Gross

Rachael Wotring

Donna McInenly

Attorney James T. Huber

Community Activist, Alan Jennings

PBS39/WLVT Lehigh Valley Public Telecommunications Corporation, Tim Fallon

Dr. Jeff A. Etchason

Attorney Malcolm J. Gross

Friend Charles B. Inlander

Retired Court Administrator, Susan T. Schellenberg

Law Clerks (in order of service)

    Christopher W. Gittinger

    Michael G. Longenhagen

    Michael J. Pawk

    Angelo T. Almonti

    John D. Reinhard

    Steven A. Litz

    Lynn Reutelhuber (now Stutzman)

    Anne C. Friday (now Beck)

Diligent *Morning Call* reporter, Debbie Garlicki

*Images* by Sharon K. Merkel

Lehigh County Historical Society

    Joseph Garrera

    Jill Youngken

Kieran McAuliffe, Graphic Artist

**Lorelei A. Broskey, Editor**

# APPENDIX

There is no room for an appendix, however:

For my Great-Grandchildren and those stalwart people who are really curious, I have opened a public Web site on the Internet containing guidelines for legal fees in handling estate matters, a poem about sentencing, hospital tax Opinions and Adjudications, a 1987 film about the creation of the Constitution featuring local lawyer talent, some bonus photographs, a "Right to Live" and "Balloon Wedding" stories, and other items that I may from time to time feel like including (tasteful suggestions welcome). The internet address is **www.trialjudgebook.com.**

I am relying upon the members of my large family to maintain the website following my demise, so that future Great-Grandchildren will be able to read and see its contents.

The cast members with speaking parts in the 1987 Bar Association film now lodged on the above referenced website, are as follows:

| | |
|---|---|
| John M. Ashcraft, III | Alexander Hamilton |
| Alan M. Black | Gouv Morris |
| Robert E. Donatelli | B. Franklin |
| William E. Doyle | Elbridge Gerry |
| Joseph A. Fitzpatrick, Jr. | James Madison, Jr. |
| A.T. Gillespie, Jr. | Wm. Saml. Johnson |
| Frank J. Madey | Governor E. Randolph |
| James B. Martin | George Washington |
| Paul A. McGinley | Thomas Mifflin |
| Michael E. Moyer | James Wilson |
| Henry S. Perkin | Wm. Patterson |
| Richard Brent Somach | Luther Martin |
| John J. Waldron | Charles Pinckney |
| Thomas A. Wallitsch | Major Jackson |
| Robert K. Young | James Mason |

Directed by Richard D. Director, Esq.

# INDEX OF NAMES

The following list of names includes those who were involved in the 28 appealed cases or noted in the narrative. My apologies to many other important people and organizations that I worked with during my judgeship. See Table of Contents for Subject Matters.

Allentown Hospital, 100
Almonti, Angelo, *5 Photo*
Anewalt, Thomas, 55
Anthony, W. Thomas, 212
Backenstoe, Judge John E., 67
Barrett, Linda C., 52
Bartel, Clyde O., 15
Barth, Larry, 66, 101, *102 Photo,*
Beltz, Tina, 67
Berrier, John G., 64
Black, Rudy, 40
Boy Scouts of America, 45
Brenner, Judge Lawrence, 139
Brocshack, Mike, 5
Brown, Robert W. 92
Burianek, Francis P., 92
Buss, Richard, 22
Butz, William B., 64
Cahn, Judge Edward N., 5
Carlisle, Rusty, 46
Coyne, Judge Martin J., 42, 48, 67
Daller, Morton F., 187
Danser, Dwight L., 187
Davison, Judge Maxwell E., 67, 224
Dickinson Law School, 43
Dickson, Dianne M., 15
Diefenderfer, Judge James N., 39, 67, 70
Dorney, Robert C., 64
Farmer, Charles, 41
Fegee, Edward H., 153
Fitzpatrick, Joseph A., 123
Fogerty, Kevin T., 15, 209
Fonzone, Charles, 32-38
Ford, Judge William C., 21
Freund, Jolin E., 22
Friday, Anne, 70
Fruhwirth, Francis A., 52
Gallager, Joseph, 44

Gardner, Judge James Knoll, 67
Giovannini, Matthew, 5
Gittinger, Christopher, 3, 43
Good Shepherd Home, 101
Griffith, Elissa J., 15
Gross, Malcolm J., 171
Grossinger, Dr. Jerome, 208
Hanna, Robert J. Jr., 171
Herring, A. Martin, 153
Heitzman, George, 131
Herman, Kent H., 78
Johnstone, Peter D.
Juvenile Court, 26, 106
Kalmbach Estate, 64 et seq.
Kantra, Emil W., 109
Knerr, David G.,123
Krouse, Gwin M., 56, 212
Lauer, Philip D., 187
Lehigh University, 64
Lehigh Valley Hospital, 100
Mackall, Paul and Evania, 65-66
Malkames, Mark, 163
Marino, Marcie, 52
Marles, Blake C., 123
Marshall, Chief Justice John, 229
McCready, Linda, Michael & Laura, 65
McGinley, Judge Carol K., 45
McLain, Erv D., 209
Mellenberg, Judge David E., 67, 98, 187
Miller, Donna M., 123
Minnesota, University of, 65
Muhlenberg Osteopathic Hospital, 101
National Judicial College, 45, 224
Orloski, Richard, 32
Orphans' Court, 14, 41, 42, 47, 48, 54, 63, 65-67, 101, 106, 146, 225
Palladino, Madaline, 109
Pavlack, Keith R., 78

Penn, William, 72
Pennsylvania, University of, 4, 43, 65
Perkin, Judge Henry S., 72
Piosa, Michael, 51
Rehnquist, U. S. Chief Justice, 224
Reibman, Judge Edward D., 45
Rochester, University of, 64
Roseberry, Catharine M., 51
Sacred Heart Hospital, 100 et seq.
Scheie, Dr. Harold G., 65-66
Schellenberg, Susan T., 21
Schmoyer, Edie, 5
Seislove, Michael, *102 Photo*
Sigmon, Mark S., 131
Simon, William, 64
Sorrentino, Matthew, 51
St. Luke's Hospital, 100 et seq.
Stauffer, Helen Z., 55
Steinberg, Judge Robert L., 50, 51, 70
Sweifel, Nellie. 44
Thompson, Anthony R., 109
Thornburgh, Governor Dick, 4
Thwaites, Jan, 42, 48, 66, 101, 104, 225
Traud, Thomas F., 92
Wallitsch, Judge Thomas A., 64
Wieand, Donald E. Jr., 163
Yost, Barbara, 7, 40, 42
Young, Carolyn, 3, *7 Photo*, 43, 46, 232
Young, Donald S., 43